LEARNING LO

BEGINNING MATHEMATICS

Part I   *"Learning Logic, Logical Games"*
Part II *"Sets, Numbers and Powers"*
Part III *"Exploration of Space and Practical Measurement"*

LEARNING LOGIC,
LOGICAL GAMES

by

Z. P DIENES

Director of the Department of Psycho-Mathematics,
University of Sherbrooke, Quebec.

and

E. W. GOLDING

Master of Method
Cowandilla Demonstration School,
South Australia.

E|S|A
in association with
UNIVERSITY OF LONDON PRESS LTD.

First published in Great Britain 1966
by The Educational Supply Association,
Harlow, Essex.

Second impression 1968
Third impression 1969
Fourth impression 1970
Fifth impression 1971

published jointly by
The Educational Supply Association,
Harlow, Essex,

and

University of London Press Ltd,
St. Paul's House, Warwick Lane,
London, EC4P 4AH

0 340 15791 7 (ULP)

© 1966 OCDL Paris

Printed in England

CONTENTS

1. INTRODUCTION

SOME THOUGHTS ABOUT MATHEMATICS AND CHILDREN

This handbook is intended for teachers of young children, and we offer no apology when we insist that the "arithmetic" of yesteryear must give way to the study of "mathematics" so early in the child's career. In this modern age it is necessary to bring up children so that they understand mathematics and its uses. It is becoming essentially a part of our culture.

This significant change is bound to have many effects, and we, as teachers, cannot continue to ignore the problems which these raise in the educational situation. It has not been found sufficient to reform the secondary school syllabus, even where this has been done, in order to prepare our children satisfactorily for what they will be called upon to do at the university. It has not even been sufficient to reform the primary school syllabus, so that they, the children, will be ready to do more serious work in the secondary school. It is becoming generally accepted that when the child first enters school, his mathematical situation must be taken seriously.

These statements may tend to give the mistaken impression that our recommendations in this field of "modern mathematics" refer only to those children who will ultimately undertake university courses. The need will be as great for those others who do not proceed as far with their formal education. It is already becoming obvious that the world of tomorrow will require its people to be "mathematically literate", even though they may not have proceeded beyond the early secondary school stage.

This booklet gives an account of the kind of experiences with which we could greet children when they first come to school, and continue to give them through the first two school grades. However, there can be no hard and fast rules laid down about what a child can, or cannot, learn during these first two years at school.

The suggestions made here are the result of a number of years' work in different parts of the world, mainly in Adelaide (South Australia), Papua New Guinea, Leicestershire (England), and Massachusetts (U. S. A.). Despite the fact that what is included here has been fairly tested, it is already quite evident that the suggestions contained in this booklet will have to be revised in the light of further experience. Some of the exercises may be found to be too difficult for the average child, and others may have to be introduced to make the course of conceptual development more complete.

1.1. *Content and organization*

This handbook is divided into three separate volumes ; the first is about the learning of logic by young children, volume 2 is about the introduction of number, through the properties of sets, and continuing up to the idea of powers, volume 3 deals briefly with the practical applications of number in situations involving measurement, weight, capacity, time, area, and so on, and suggests an early approach to geometry.

It has not been thought necessary to include a section on approaches to learning the so-called "number facts" and relationships that are necessary to every child, as these are well known and admirably handled by most teachers at this stage [1].

It must not be thought that the course to be presented to the children should follow the sequence of this subdivision, with logic preceding number, and so on. The logical work, for instance, is intended to grow side by side with the other aspects, though it is natural that very little measurement will be possible until some ideas of number have developed. But, as soon as this has taken place, many practical situations should be engineered in which children can be encouraged to use their newly-developed notions of number.

In the appendix a certain number of "games" are provided. These are not intended for the children to read and follow as, clearly, the vocabulary and possibly even the reading ability of children in the early grades will not permit them on the whole to read, interpret, and carry out the instructions. They could, of course, be used by older children or by intending teachers making up lesson plans. In presenting the instructions on sets and measurement, we have given these in a manner which should suggest plans for lessons, or for parts of lessons, but the actual details must be determined by the teachers.

1.2. *The classroom situation*

Drastic changes in the mathematics curriculum would not be possible if we were to retain the traditional classroom procedures and atmosphere at the same time. In fact, we hope that teachers will endeavour to change "a teaching situation" into "a learning situation".

1. See especially the Stern Apparatus ESA (Publishers note).

It must be emphasized that, with the kind of approach suggested here, far less "whole class teaching" will take place. Much of the work will be done by children working in small groups, or even individually. These groups can be formed by the teacher, or she may allow the children to form themselves into groups. They will work together quite happily, especially if the work is not spoiled for them by the creation of a reward-punishment system. Children are essentially interested in finding out new things about their world, and we do not have to spoil this interest by introducing compulsions or rewards for work well done. A smile from the teacher, or a pat on the back, is quite sufficient reward for a task well completed.

If we work in this way, the children will be encouraged to learn mathematics for its own sake, and not in order to excel or outdo their classmates in competition. Groups will form, will change in composition, and re-form, as some children learn more quickly than others. There will be a place for individual work, too, and there will be times when it will be more profitable for the whole class to work together. A case in point occurs in the study of sets. Sets are probably most satisfactorily introduced by considering the children in the class as possible members of any sets. In other words the universal set can, in the first place, be defined as the set of all the children in the class. At a later stage, too, equivalence games are most easily played by using the children themselves. When the question is asked, "Are there more chairs than children, or more children than chairs?" the children will readily find out, if they are allowed to do so, by trying to sit on the chairs. If all the children are able to sit down, one to a seat, and there are some empty chairs, then, of course, there are more chairs than children—and nobody needs to know the exact numbers of children or chairs. In these situations the joint experience of the class, or at any rate of a large part of the class, will be beneficial. So no hard and fast rules can be laid down as to whether individual work, small group work, or whole class work is the best way to handle a situation. It must, in the last resort, be left to the teacher to choose what he feels is the best approach in the situation in which he finds himself. Very frequently, when a new aspect is to be introduced, the class will be best taken as a whole. This activity may not last long, for it may be found that progress has been so varied that the next stage must be taken in groups—and this may be so even before one lesson has been completed.

An important part of learning takes place by discussions among the children. To illustrate this let us take the case of a logical game, with a Venn Diagram being completed on the floor. If a child puts a piece in the wrong place, it is much less useful for the teacher to interfere than for another child to correct it. The two children can argue the matter out on the same level, and the child who thinks the piece has been wrongly placed will usually argue quite forcibly, while the other child argues the point back again. The rules of the game are quite simple enough for the truth to prevail eventually in such an argument. This is very good training, as it is very much better to encourage children to appeal to the truth in a situation than to appeal to the authority of some person who is a purveyor of truth, such as a teacher.

When children are encouraged to discuss not only what they are doing but also what they believe they have discovered, quite naturally there will be a certain amount of noise in the classroom. However, there is no need to allow excessive noise to prevent learning from taking place, or to interrupt the activities of other classes. The teacher must realize that he is still in charge, and must insist that necessary noise be limited. But, it is amazing how much noise a child is able to support, while yet doing a considerable amount of delicate thinking. It is usually the teacher who is "driven mad" by the excessive amount of noise, and not the children. On the other hand, just as the teacher must get used to a more noisy situation, the children must learn to consider others. We have found that, with a little "give and take", this problem is usually solved satisfactorily.

If the children learn best by activity methods, and if discussion will help such learning, the teacher must adjust to the new situation ; while, if children are to learn in the usual school situation with other classes nearby, they must limit the volume of noise that they create.

In the implementation of a scheme of learning such as described in this handbook, there will be a great amount of concrete material to be handled by the children and by the teacher. Taken in conjunction with group and individual work, this calls for a considerable amount of organization ; if the activities and the materials are not properly organized there will be chaos, loss of time, and poor learning conditions. One way of making sure that every child knows exactly what to start with at the beginning of a lesson is to put a diagram on the blackboard, with the names of children or groups beside each section of the diagram. Sketches are sometimes necessary because children cannot yet read instructions : thus we might use three interlocking circles for a Venn Diagram, or a quick sketch of some blocks to show an exchanging game. The materials, too, must have a definite place in the classroom, or in the corridor, where the children are able to reach them, so that, before the mathematics lesson, the teacher can simply ask certain responsible children to collect materials, put them where they will be needed, and distribute cards. At the end of the lesson, children may again be asked to check materials, pack and replace them tidily in the cupboards.

Once such an organization has been established there seems to be no trouble in getting the class started, but it certainly does need organizing ; it will not happen by itself. Except at such times as when a new aspect is to be introduced, teachers will be well advised to "stagger" the changeover periods of the groups or of the individual children so that the beginning of a lesson sees most children continuing an activity of which they have some knowledge, while only a few must be introduced to something new. This, too, calls for considerable ability as an organizer.

It is not possible for a traditionally trained teacher to pass over to this kind of mathematics without a certain amount of heart-searching, and a consequent change in attitude. For example, the idea that the truth is the authority, and not the teacher, is something rather difficult for some teachers to accept. Children themselves are accustomed simply to "ask the teacher". It is very tempting to interfere with children when they are making mistakes, and tell them how to do things when they don't know. It is quite difficult to stand by and watch a child fumbling away, not being able to solve a problem, when all the teacher would have to do would be to say, "Look, put it over there," and it would be done. This, of course, would rob this child of the benefit arising from that particular learning situation in which he is expected to discover for himself what the solution is. By solving it for himself, he has the opportunity of fixing the solution in his mind very much more clearly and permanently than if the teacher merely tells him what to do.

In addition teachers should try to remember that the ways in which they think are not necessarily the ways in which the children think. In fact, child-thinking is very different from adult-thinking, and even different children seem to think problems out in different ways. There is no single way to solve a problem. Very often a child, given the opportunity, will suggest an avenue of attack for a problem which is not the avenue that the teacher himself would have chosen—in fact, the line of attack might seem to him to be entirely wrong. The best educational approach in such a case would have the teacher avoid saying, "that is wrong : do it this way," and have him join with the child in an investigation of what is entailed in the child's suggestion. A discussion, or a joint piece of discovery, could then follow, with the child's approach examined for what it is worth. If it is a good one, and if the child is intelligent enough to follow it up, he may convince the teacher. If this does not happen, and the child goes on fumbling and finding that the method is not particularly successful, then it will be time for the teacher to suggest that some other line of attack might be advisable.

It should not be thought, because it is suggested that children should not be unduly interfered with, that this implies that they should always be left entirely to their own devices. Occasional helpful suggestions from the teacher are a very necessary part of the learning process, but these should never take the form of commands. A child's mistake should not be pointed out to him in so many words, even though it be apparent to the teacher. The consequences of the mistakes should become apparent to the child. He must realise his result is absurd, and it will then be borne in on him that his approach was incorrect. It is very much better to discover one's own mistakes than to be told about them by someone else, and in the process it is found that more is learned about the structure of the problem. If the child is told, "No. It is wrong ; you don't do it this way. Do it that way," he learns nothing about the problem, for he has not had any personal active experience of handling it.

It is extremely difficult to give an idea of how such a class of young five-, six-, and seven-year-olds proceeds, without actually showing it in action. It is hoped that as many teachers as possible, who intend to implement the suggestions contained in this handbook, will have the opportunity of going to some other schools where these new methods are already employed. If she lives in an area where schools are already practising these methods, she will not find this difficult to achieve. If she lives far away from such schools, then she could probably still arrange to travel to another area and to stay for two or three days, watching the learning situation develop in these schools. The International Study Group for Mathematics Learning has a number of centres in different parts of the world, and these centres are designed to carry out research into the fundamental educational problems of mathematical learning, as well as being designed to help teachers put these ideas into practice. Interested teachers should be in constant contact with their nearest centre.

2. LOGIC

2.1. FUNDAMENTAL IDEAS

A considerable part of mathematics is concerned with the study of numbers. Numbers have no concrete existence such as the objects have that we see around us. Numbers are properties, just as colours, shapes, sizes, textures are properties. There is no such object as "a large", but there are large objects. Largeness is a property which does not have a concrete existence. So is colour ; there is no object which is "a blue", but there are blue objects. Sizes, colours, shapes, etc., are properties, or attributes, that refer to objects. Number is a property which refers to sets of objects. No object can have the property "two". A set of objects can have the property "two". So, before studying number, sets of objects must clearly be studied. It must be realized that sets refer to objects and numbers refer to sets. The objects are the bedrock of experience ; as soon as we start grouping objects and forming sets of them, we are already organizing this bedrock experience in our minds, because we need to sort out our primary experiences in order to make some sense of them. Sets are already abstractions. One way of proceeding to sort out our sets is to put them in "equivalence classes", classifying them according to the number of members there are in them. All sets with a membership of one, are grouped together into the 1-class. All sets with two members in them are put into the 2-class, and so on. All sets belonging to the same classification have the same "number-property".

There are several ways of defining sets. One way would be to enumerate all the members. This might be tedious if there are a great number of members as, for example, all the inhabitants of California. The more usual way of defining larger sets is by deciding on the attributes that its members must have. But just deciding on the attributes is not enough. For example, if we say, "the inhabitants of California", do we mean only human inhabitants, or do we include some animals, and, if so, which kind, etc.? We must decide on a *fundamental set*, or *universal set* in which we will put the members of our set. This universal set in our example would be "the set of living human beings", in which case the property "being an inhabitant of California" will select a certain definite set of people from the entire human family. But even so we must be careful that the criterion is in every case decisive. For example, we must make it clear what we mean by inhabitant. Do we mean "permanent resident" or "anyone who happens to be in California on a certain day"? Once the criterion has been sufficiently refined so as to enable us to state for any member of the universal set whether it does or does not have the attribute in question, then that attribute defines a set.

There are certain relationships between sets, such as one set being included in another, or one set having no common member with another, or one set having exactly the same members as another (in which case it is not really "another"!), which will need study. There are also *operations* we can perform on sets and so generate other sets.

For example, we could consider the operation of "finding the common part of two sets". Consider the sets defined by the attributes :

"earning less than $10.000 a year",   "inhabitants of California".

Each attribute defines a set of people. The set of those people possessing both attributes will form the common part, or intersection, of the two sets defined by the separate attributes. This "intersection set" or "common part set" will consist of people who possess the attribute :

"earning less than $10.000 a year *and* being an inhabitant of California".

So when we join two attributes by the word "and", we form the intersection of the sets defined by the separate attributes.

We could also consider the operation of "uniting two sets". If we wanted to put together all the people "earning less than $10.000 a year" with all the people who are "inhabitants of California", then we should form the *union* of the two separate sets. What attribute is possessed by members of our union-set? Clearly, it is

"either earning less than $10.000 a year or being an inhabitant of California".

so long as the "either... or" is taken in the inclusive sense ; i.e., it includes all Californians earning less than $10.000 as well as all other Californians, as well as all non-Californians earning less than $10.000 a year. So when we join two attributes by the words "either... or", we form the union of the sets defined by the separate attributes.

There is another very simple set-operation which is extremely important. It is the forming of the complementary set. For example, the complementary set of the set of people earning less than $10.000 a year is the set of people earning $10.000 or more a year. The complementary set of Californians is the set of non-Californians. To obtain the attribute applicable to the complement of a set, we must put the word "not" in front of the word defining our set. For example, if all the objects in a certain room are taken to form the universal set, then the attribute "red" defines the set of red objects in that room. The attribute "not red" defines the complement of the set of red objects, this set consisting of all the objects in the room which are not members of the "red" set.

The study of the relationships between attributes as expressed by "connectives" such as "and", "either... or", "not", and so on, and the study of the relationships between such connectives, is known as the attribute calculus. In this guide, methods are described by means of which children from the age of five upwards can learn to handle the attribute calculus.

2.2. THE ATTRIBUTE BLOCKS [1]

Young children learn best from their own, not other people's, experiences. The logical relationships that we might wish children to learn, should therefore be embodied in observable relationships between distinguishable attributes such as colour, shape, etc. This technique has been used for some time for the testing of logical thinking (concept formation) ; it was probably first used systematically by the Russian psychologist Vygotsky. William Hull was the first to show in practical ways [2] that five-year-olds could indeed engage in some high order logical thinking, provided the tasks were suitably chosen and adjusted to the stage of development of such young children, and provided that great care was taken that excessive verbalism did not stand in the way of the concept formation. The blocks to be described here are a slightly varied form of the blocks used by Hull for these first experiments ; some of the games described are almost as they were played by the original experimental group ; others are developments of these games, some developed by children themselves ; and yet others, such as the transformation games and the disjunction games, are quite new. The instructions given for the games are largely based on experimentation with 5- to 7-year-old children in South Australia, but it should be noted that some of the experimentation took place in as widely separated points as Quebec, Boston, Hawaii, Leicestershire (England), Geneva, Paris, Surrey (England), California, the Philippines, and New Guinea.

The attribute blocks consist of the following set :

large thick red square,	large thick blue square,	large thick yellow square,
large thick red oblong,	large thick blue oblong,	large thick yellow oblong,
large thick red triangle,	large thick blue triangle,	large thick yellow triangle,
large thick red circle,	large thick blue circle,	large thick yellow circle,

1. The attribute blocks (or logical blocks) are obtainable from the Educational Supply Association Ltd. Pinnacles, Harlow, Essex, England, or from S. O. Wainwright, 15, Stanley Ave, Blair Atholl S. A., Australia.
2. "*Concept work with young children*", Bulletin of the International Study Group for Mathematics Learning, Vol. I, no. 2, 1963.

large thin red square,	large thin blue square,	large thin yellow square,
large thin red oblong,	large thin blue oblong,	large thin yellow oblong,
large thin red triangle,	large thin blue triangle,	large thin yellow triangle,
large thin red circle,	large thin blue circle,	large thin yellow circle,
small thick red square,	small thick blue square,	small thick yellow square,
small thick red oblong,	small thick blue oblong,	small thick yellow oblong,
small thick red triangle,	small thick blue triangle,	small thick yellow triangle,
small thick red circle,	small thick blue circle,	small thick yellow circle,
small thin red square,	small thin blue square,	small thin yellow square,
small thin red oblong,	small thin blue oblong,	small thin yellow oblong,
small thin red triangle,	small thin blue triangle,	small thin yellow triangle,
small thin red circle,	small thin blue circle,	small thin yellow circle.

It will be seen that there are four variables :

(1) size,   (2) thickness,   (3) colour,   (4) shape.

The size and the thickness variables have two values each ; i.e., large and small for the size, thick and thin for the thickness. The colour variable has three values : red, blue and yellow ; the shape variable has four values : square, oblong, triangle, and circle[1]. Each piece in the set has four "names", as indicated in the above list. Children will soon learn to name the pieces, as well as to produce out of the set any piece fully named. Familiarity with the names is an essential prerequisite to the playing of most of the games described in this guide.

Important warning. It is extremely important to allow children a considerable amount of free play with this, as with any other mathematical instructional material. If suggestions to play games are met with a negative response from any child, such a child should be allowed to go on "playing out" his own imagination and creativity. There will always be enough children in a class who want to play "games" to ensure that this activity will eventually seem desirable to all children in the class. The appendix (page 56) gives details of a number of such games.

3. THE DIFFERENCE GAMES

3.1. *The one-difference game*

Any two blocks in any one set of attribute blocks are different from each other in at least one way. Such a difference might be a difference in size, a difference in thickness, a difference in colour, or a difference in shape. Blocks may, of course, differ from one another in more than one way. For example, a large thick red square is different from a large thin red square in thickness only. These blocks are different

---

   1. Rhombi are now used instead of "oblongs" in Australia.

from each other in one way only.   A large thick red square is different from a large thin blue square in thickness and in colour.   These blocks are different from each other in just two ways.   To encourage children to become conscious of such differences and similarities, the difference games are introduced.

One child puts down any piece out of the set.   The next child puts down a piece which is different from the first piece in one attribute only.   This difference might be size only, or thickness only, or colour only, or shape only.   The next player, which would be the first player if there are only two children playing, puts down a third piece, which differs from the second piece in one attribute only. The game goes on in this way until all, or nearly all, the pieces in the set have been placed in a row.

A "One-difference" game

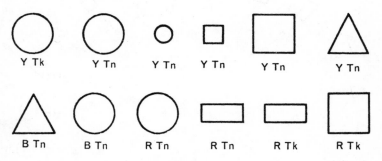

Figure 1

Each player has the right to challenge the previous player.   This means that if a player believes that the previous player put down a piece which did not differ in one attribute only from the piece before, he can say so.   If he wins his challenge, he gains a point.   If he wrongly challenges a previous player, he loses a point.   Each success-ful, i.e., unchallenged placement of a piece gains a point.   So points can be gained by

(1) playing a piece according to the rules.

(2) discovering that the opponent has broken the rules.

In the latter case, if the challenge is substantiated, the player who made the error naturally loses the point that he gained for the place-ment of the piece which had now been proved to have been an error. The child with the largest number of points wins the game.   The fact that the players are allowed to challenge each other encourages them to concentrate not only on their own moves but also on the moves of the other players.

19

The next "one-difference" game can be played by making a "pile" instead of making a "train" and the children should be aware that they can build in either way, but not in the same game, yet.

Returning to the "train": after the children have been playing for some time, they might try "joining on", which means that they will build their train in a circle, and when they discover a block which will fit, they may end the game by completing the circle. It must be understood that, to do this, they must find a block which is different in one way from the last one played, and is also different in one way from the first block played.

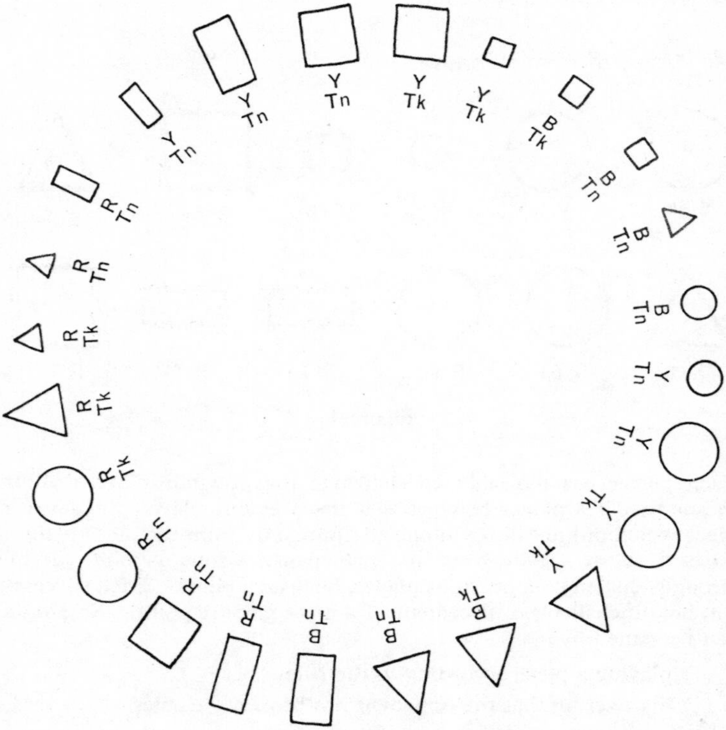

Figure 2

Much harder is to try to build the "train" in the shape of a figure "8", as the centre piece must be different in one way from each of four pieces, so this game should be left until the children have become adept at the one-difference games.

3.2. *The two-difference game and elaborations*

An obvious elaboration of the one-difference game would be a two-difference game. Again, the first player puts down any piece out of the set. The second player puts down a piece which differs from the first piece in two and only two attributes. For example, if a large thick red square is put down by the first player, the next player might put down a small thin red square. In this case the second piece differs from the first piece in size and thickness. It could, of course, have differed from the first piece in any other two attributes. For example, a large thin blue square would have been correct as the second piece, or a large thick yellow circle. Again children will be allowed to challenge each other, each player having the right to challenge the previous player. The same procedure applies as before as regards the gaining or losing of points.

Naturally, this game can be extended to a three-difference game or even to a four-difference game.

3.3. *Mixed difference games*

Some of the brighter children will want to make up more difficult games, such as, "mixed-difference" games. They may decide to start with the "one-two-difference" game, which is a mixture of the first two of these games. The first player will, as usual, play any block, and the next player must play a block which is different in one way, the following player must play a piece which is different in two ways, the next player one which is different in one way, and so on. The player must remember, not only what he must play, but also whether he is a "one-difference" player, or a "two-difference" player this time.

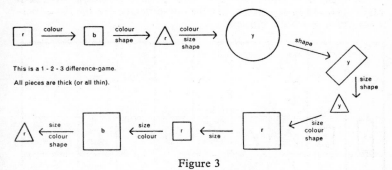

Figure 3

When this game is well understood, the players might decide to play the "one-two-three difference" game, in which, after the first player has played his block, the second player makes a one-difference change, the third player a two-difference change, the fourth a three-difference change, the fifth a one-difference change again, and so on. If this game is played with any other than three players, it becomes more interesting, and more difficult, as the player must always be thinking of the kind of change he must make next time. (With three players, after the first round, each player has to make the same kind of move each time, as there are three variations.)

Children should be encouraged to make up games such as these in any way they wish, and to play them—competitively or not, as they decide.

3.4. *The domino game*

The domino game is a far more difficult version of the one-difference and the two-difference games, as it is played in two directions at the same time. We have found it best to play this game on a "square grid", each square being made large enough to hold the largest block in our set.

The game is played in one direction as a one-difference game, and this is the way in which it is started. The first player places any block in any square he decides, but it is best to start somewhere about the middle of our grid (which may be drawn in chalk on the floor, or may be more permanently laid out on a piece of material, which can be rolled up and used again). Now, if the second player decides to make the second block "one-different" from the first, he must place this block either in the next square to the right, or in the next square to the left, of the first block, as we are playing the "one-difference" game in this direction. However, he may choose to play the "two-difference" game, and, if so, he must place the next block either in the next square towards us, or in the next square away from us, as we are playing the "two-difference" game in this direction. So each player plays in turn, using either the one-difference or the two-difference game, as it suits himself.

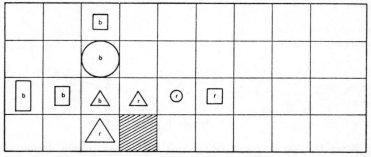

Figure 4   *The beginnings of a domino game. The shaded area could be filled, for example, by a big blue triangle.*

When this game is played competitively the players get one point for every difference that they make. That is, if the player plays in the one-difference direction, and is not challenged, he gets one point, or one counter, but, if he plays in the two-difference direction, and plays the right block, he gets two points, as he has made two changes. The same values go to the challenger, who gets the same number of points as the player would have got, if he had not made a mistake—but the challenger who makes a wrong challenge loses the same number of points as he would have gained, had he been successful.

The problem comes, of course, when trying to fill a "corner" or a "gap" because the player has to make, perhaps, a one-difference change in one direction, while, at the same time, making a two-difference change in the other direction. If he can do this successfully, he gains three points. If there is a "gap" in the middle of four blocks, already placed, and he can find a block which fits into it, he can gain six points in all, but these moves are seldom possible. A challenger can gain or lose the same number of points in each case.

3.5. *The contradiction game*

This is a game which is played when players are used to playing the domino game. For it, we will need two other kinds of markers, so let us use a stone for one and a piece of chalk for the other.

As we are playing two games at the one time—the one-difference and the two-difference games—there will come a time when there is a space which it is impossible to fill. For example, suppose that our middle row in the one-difference direction has, as usual, a normal one-difference sequence along it and that a player has played a two-difference piece from the centre block. The next player may also play a two-difference move, using, not the block next to the centre, but the next one ; so we will have two blocks in our second horizontal row, with a gap between them. Along this second row we are playing another one-difference game, as we are in all the rows parallel to the first one-difference row. If we look carefully at these two blocks, we may find that there are three, or even four, differences between them, so it will be impossible to find a piece which will fill the gap. If a player, when it comes his turn, can find such an impossible situation, he can put a stone in that square, saying that it is not possible to fill it. If he proves to be right, he gets five points for finding the impossibility.

As our game proceeds, and we use many of the blocks, there will be another kind of problem. Now we may have a gap which could have been filled, but we have no piece left which could fill it. If a player, when it comes his turn to play, says, "This gap cannot be filled with any of the blocks that we have left" and puts a piece of chalk in the place, he can get three points. Of course, the player using either the stone or the chalk, can be challenged, and the challenger can get the same number of points, if successful, or may lose the same number of points if not successful.

Children should always be encouraged to look out for these impossibilities or absurdities in all games.

A further refinement would be to start building upwards. The differences upwards, i.e. when a tower is made of the pieces, could be three. In other words, it would be possible to put a piece on top of any other which differs from the lower piece in three attributes. Our cross-attribute would then acquire not just one but several layers. Of course, each layer must itself be a valid cross-attribute—in other words, an attempt would be being made to construct a three-dimensional cross-attribute. It would seem, at first, that such a feat would be quite beyond the powers of five to seven year old children. Although there are some young children that cannot rise to such heights of complexity, yet there are some who can. It would be wrong to deprive able children from the exercise of their capabilities by not giving them the chance to stretch themselves in this fashion.

It has been found that a "four-difference direction" is easier to combine with a "one-difference direction". Children can see that a piece is "very" different from another piece by simply looking at the two pieces. They can also more readily discover an error, because there will be an attribute which the two pieces have in common, and they will know that under this rule such a situation is not allowed.

Teachers are warned against insisting on children enumerating the differences prematurely. Children acquire quite an uncanny power of discrimination in these games which seldom fails them. The pairing game will be introduced to bring these intuitions to the level of conscious awareness.

There is an interesting extension of the domino-game which has sometimes been played successfully with young children. This extension becomes possible when all the pieces have been used up and children might wish to move the pieces around that have already been placed. In this case children can be told that they can buy a piece or even two or three pieces, the price of a piece being the number of differences with which this piece is joined to the remaining body of blocks. Sometimes it is possible to make a "profit" in this way, although sometimes one might suffer a loss. One way of playing the game is by stipulating that each child must decide just how many pieces he is going to buy for "investment" purposes, up to say a maximum of three, and having bought these pieces, he is then at liberty to place them in any way he likes in conformity with the rules of the game being played. In this way a child might lose on one piece, but this loss could be offset by gains on the other pieces.

24

4. THE PAIRING GAMES

4.1. *The eight-piece game*

In the pairing game eight pieces are selected. We select three attri-butes with two values for each e.g. we might take shape, colour and size, and select two shapes, two colours and two sizes. The two shapes might be square and triangle, the two colours might be red and blue, and the two sizes must, of course, be large and small. If every com-bination of these attributes is to be represented in the game there will, of course, be eight pieces. The first player in the game puts any two of the eight pieces together in a pair. The second player is required to construct another pair *in the same way* as the first pair. By this is meant that the differences between the members of the second pair must be the same differences as the differences between the members of the first pair. For example if the first pair consists of the large red square and the small red square, then only the size is varied as between the members of the first pair. The second pair must be constructed in a similar fashion. For example the second pair could be the large blue square and the small blue square. It could not be, for example, the large blue square and the small blue triangle because in this case, not only the size but also the shape would have been varied between members of the pairs. The second pair can of course be challenged by the third player whose eventual task is to construct again a similar pair. In the third pair the same differences and similarities between the members of the pairs must exist as between the members of the first and the second pairs. If the third pair has been correctly constructed, then the fourth pair will automatically be correctly put together. The fourth player will have, of course, the chance to challenge the third player. Turns can be taken for making the first pair, so as to make the chances of winning points as even as possible.

4.2. *Making all the pairings*

There are exactly seven ways of making such pairings. The point of the game could be the eventual construction of all seven such pairings. Each such pairing consists naturally, of four pairs, each pair being in each case constructed in a similar manner to each other pair in that pairing. The game could be played by stipulating that no pair must be made twice so if any two pieces have been together once, those two pieces must never be together again. Any person who puts a pair together that has already been together in a previous pairing can be challenged and if the challenge is substantiated then such a player will lose a point. In this way all the seven pairings can be constructed and the scores totalled up. The highest scorer wins the game.

25

4.3. *Recording*

It is extremely difficult to play the above game without some effective method of recording. The problem can be left to the children and they will usually record at first by simply drawing the pairings that have been constructed. After a while, a more systematic and methodical recording will emerge. If it is regarded as necessary, a more methodical type of recording may actually be suggested. Even record cards may be supplied on which the seven columns are put in three rows.

	First pairing					Fifth pairing	
Different in shape	yes	no	no	yes	no	yes	yes
Different in colour	no	yes	no	yes	yes	no	yes
Different in size	no	no	yes	no	yes	yes	yes

The first pairing recorded on the record card is :

The fifth pairing would be, for example :

Figure 5   and so on.

In the columns can be placed "Yes" or "no" or ticks and crosses, or whatever the children may decide. Each column will then represent a pairing. It will then be possible to see whether or not a pairing has already been constructed and so a challenge can be substantiated without argument. The difficulty of resolving such arguments without recording would in itself be a powerful inducement to get the children to resort to some recording.

4.4. *The sixteen-piece game*

If instead of three attributes, the fourth attribute of thickness is introduced then there will be 16 pieces and in each pairing there will be eight pairs.   There will in this case be fifteen different possible pairings.   This is rather a difficult task and only the abler children will be able to carry through the fifteen different pairings.   It is, of course, possible to restrict matters to two attributes instead of three, e.g. shape and color, each having two values.   In this case there are only four pieces in the set and there are only three possible pairings. It has been found by experience that it is best to start with the eight-piece set and then possibly to proceed to the four-piece set, then to the sixteen-piece set.   The game can be generalized to other attributes, such as hair-colour, eye-colour, sex and so on, so that the children in the class can themselves be paired.   Supposing we take fair and dark children, blue-eyed and brown-eyed children and boys and girls.   In this case there will be eight different children in each set. They can be asked to pair themselves into pairs and find out in how many ways they can do this so that no pair is constructed more than once.   There will, of course, be seven pairings and in each pairing there will be four pairs.   Such exercises will help children to transfer their logical thinking from the blocks to other situations.   The problem can be put to them to invent still further situations in which the same, or similar games, can be played.

For example, pictures of "skinny" and "fat" children, "curly-haired" and "straight-haired" children, boys and girls, will provide a set of playing cards which can be used in much the same way as the attribute blocks.   Or, of course, any other attributes can be used.

5. THE NEGATION GAMES

5.1. *The simple halving negation game*

The purpose of this game is to teach the children the principle of contradiction, i.e. for example, if something is in a certain place, it cannot be somewhere else as well.   Two teams are chosen and they are seated at either end of a table.   Let us call them teams A and B. A screen or some object is put across the table so that each side can place some blocks near the screen so that they are invisible to the other side.   Each side should have 24 blocks chosen at random out of the set.   The game begins by, say, team A asking for a block from team B.   Asking means that all four attributes must be correctly named.   If such a block is in fact in team B's part of the table then this block must be handed over.   Then team B asks for a block from team A.   Each side takes it in turn to ask for a block from the other side.   Any block that has already been named, asked for and passed over cannot be subsequently asked for.   The game can be terminated by one side having a certain number more pieces than the other side.

It is found that in the beginning many children will ask for a piece which they can see on their own side.   They do not realize that if a

27

piece is on their own side, that same piece cannot also be on the other side. Nor can they realize that if it is not on their side then it must inevitably be on the other side. In this game there is the germ of an implication. Children learn that if every piece is either here or there, they can conclude that if it is here then it is not there, and also if it is not here then it is there. These two deductions from the strict "either-or" situation of every piece being either here OR there but not in both places is an important logical step. Children will very soon learn to play this game and as soon as they reach the stage when no further errors are made, i.e. no pieces are asked for which are not on the other side, then the game should be discontinued.

5.2. *The hiding game*

This is perhaps a somewhat more difficult version of the Negation Game which can be played by a small group of children. One particular child is the one that hides a piece while the other children are not lookir g. The piece is hidden under a box or in somebody's pocket and then the other children have to determine which piece it is. At first children will try to make a tidy set of piles out of the remaining pieces and thereby determine which piece, is missing. This should not be discouraged as this is the children's way of trying to make order out of apparent chaos. If and when they get good at this by rearranging the pieces left on the table then it should be suggested to them that they should try and guess the missing piece without touching the pieces. As long as they are able to see all the pieces on the table with the exception of the missing one, they should be able to do the arranging mentally. This is a greater challenge and becomes more fun once the method of physical arrangement has become too easy.

To make the game more challenging more than one piece may be hidden. Children will soon find that, for example, if three particular pieces of all three colours but of the same shape, size and thickness are hidden, all small, thin triangles could be taken, i.e. a small thin red triangle, a small thin blue triangle and a small thin yellow triangle. This is much more difficult to detect than if three pieces are taken at random because when the tidy piles are made, even mentally, there is no particular pile which is deficient. This depends, of course, on how the piles are made. The game can be played in such a way that either one, or two, or three pieces can be hidden, or perhaps an indeterminate number of pieces (including possibly no pieces) are hidden. It must then be determined whether any pieces are hidden at all, and if they are, how many, and in this case, which ones. Children are well able to learn how to do this without touching any of the pieces.

5.3. *The "not" game*

In this game a child picks up any piece and asks the other children in his group to say all the things that the piece chosen is not. For example, the child chooses a small thin red square. This piece is not large, it is not thick, it is not blue, it is not yellow, it is not an oblong, it is not a triangle and it is not a circle. But it is also not a red triangle, it is not a thick red square, and so on. Eventually children will begin to state attributes that are not possessed by any member of the set of the attribute blocks, for example that it is not black, it is not a rabbit, it is not to be eaten, and so on. This should be allowed. In this way the enormous extent of what something is "not" will be made accessible to the children.

Another form of this game is for a child to try to enumerate all the things that he is not. Or he can alternate between things that he is and things that he is not. The first mistake puts him out of the game, and the person who spotted the mistake then begins to enumerate the properties that he is and those that he is not in rapid succession. For other "not" games please see the appendix page 75.

6. TWENTY-QUESTIONS GAMES

6.1. *Game with answers only*

For this game there should preferably be some symbols drawn or painted on pieces of wood or cardboard and some words such as "large", "small", "thick", "thin" and "not". The colours red, blue and yellow can be simply painted or drawn in coloured crayons on pieces of wood or cardboard to act as symbols, and the shapes may also be drawn in the form of actual squares, circles, oblongs and triangles. A large number of these will be necessary. One child should be appointed as leader and he will ask another child to think of a piece without saying which piece it is. The leader will ask the rest of the children in the group to ask questions such as, "Is it red?", "Is it blue?", "Is it an oblong?" "Is it large?" and so on. The person who thought, of the piece will then say "Yes" or "No" as the case may be. Each time a question has been asked and the answer has been given the answer is put down on the table ; for exemple, if the question was "Is it blue?" and the answer is "No", then "Not blue" is put down on the table as the information which is now available. Or if it is asked: "Is it large?" and the answer is "yes", then the word "large" is put down on the table, and so on. It will at first be found that children will ask far too many questions. In other words, they do not make full use of the information. This should be allowed e.g. the question might be asked "Is it large?" and then "large" is put on the table. Another child might ask "Is it small?" In this case "not small" will go on the table. It will not necessarily be realized that "large" implies "not small", or that "not small" implies "large", simply because every piece is either large or small, and so if it is not one of these then it must be the other ; or if it is one of these then it cannot be the other. Of course, if the Negation Game has been played it is more likely that such distinctions or relationships will be perceived. The first person who makes use of the information and picks up the right piece can be the next person to choose a piece, and the game starts again.

6.2. *Game with answers and deductions*

A slightly more sophisticated form of the game would be to use two tables, one as a *deduction table* and one as *an answer table*. The answers to the questions go on to the answer table and if anyone makes a correct deduction such deductions go on the deduction table, e.g. if it is asked "is it thin?" and the answer is "no" then "not thin" goes up on the answer table. If somebody says "Well, it must be thick, then" at this point the leader of the game puts the word "thick" on the deduction table. In order to make it quite easy to determine the chosen piece from the deduction table, any "positive" answers on the answer table should also be placed on the deduction table ; e.g. if it is asked "Is it yellow?" and the answer is "yes" then "yellow" will go on the answer table, but in this case it is suggested that "yellow" should also go on the deduction table. This merely means that we are not requiring children consciously to make such a deduction as: "if it is yellow then it is yellow", but only such deductions as : "if it is not large then it is small", or "if it is not thick then it is thin", or perhaps the more complicated deductions "if it is not red and it is not blue then it is yellow". If the words "not red" as well as the words "not blue" are on the answer table and then somebody says : "Well, it must be yellow", then at that stage the leader may pick up a yellow symbol and put this on the deduction table. If this procedure is followed the deduction table will give the most coherent and concise account of the information to date. The answer table will rapidly accumulate a great deal of redundant information such as "thick", "not thin", "not yellow", "not red", "blue", etc. Again the first person to pick out the correct piece should be the next person to think up the piece for the next round.

In this game children learn to make use of information. Some questions are better suited to yield optimum information than others. Children might ask: "Is it a blue square?" If it is not, then all the information they have gained is that it is one of 44 pieces, instead of one of 48. If it is a blue square (but this is unlikely), then the "gamble" has paid off, and they have enormously narrowed down the field. It is unlikely that many children would do such conceptual "gambling" before a great deal of experience has been accumulated by them on this kind of procedure. The question "Is it blue?"

narrows down the 48 possibilities to either 32 or 16, depending on the answer to the question, and so is less of a gamble.

Children will go on asking questions to which they should already know the answers from previous questions, i.e. they will ask redundant questions. These types of questions will gradually be eliminated if the game is played competitively, group competing against group. Twenty-questions games are a very good introduction to information theory on a practical level, and children who have played such games will be in a much more favourable position to understand what is meant by the "measuring" of information than those that have had no personal experience of extracting information out of situations in the most economical manner.

6.3. *The set guessing game* [1]

Let us suppose that the pieces have been set out in orderly fashion as a six by eight matrix, as described in the matrix game (see next game). One child can think of a set, characterized by, let us say, the conjunction of two attributes. For example, he might think of large triangles. Then every large triangle is an exemplar of his set, a member of his set, and every piece which is not a large triangle, is not a member. For example, small triangles would not be members, nor any large pieces that were not triangles. Two or three children would take it in turns to point at pieces and ask the child who thought of the set if such pieces were members or not. A "yes" answer would perhaps be denoted by placing a green counter on such a piece, a "no" answer by placing a red counter on such a piece. The first child who can either name the set by its attributes or pick up all the members of the set all at once (but no others!) wins the game, and this child will think of the next set.

At first children guess wildly, not making any use whatever of any information that could be obtained from the green and red pieces that have already been placed on the pieces. An occasional remark by the teacher such as "You are not having much luck over there, are you?" might induce the children to think about the problem. Naturally the child who "guesses" the correct set in the smallest number of questions becomes the "champion", and it will be a challenge to see if he can be beaten, i. e. if it is possible to "guess" the set another time in even a smaller number of questions.

It will not be expected that very sophisticated strategies will arise in the beginning. With sufficient practice, however, children will learn to make use of information. For example, if a large yellow thin triangle is a "yes" piece, it is a good strategy to vary only one attribute at a time and enquire whether a large red thin triangle is a

1. This game is due to Jerome Bruner. See *"A study of thinking"*, Bruner, Goodnow and Austin, Wiley; New York, 1956. Bruner used cards and adult subjects.

"yes" piece or not. If it is not, then it must have been the yellow that made the difference, and the word "yellow" must form part of the set to be guessed. Equally, if the latter piece is a "yes" piece, then the colour cannot have made any difference, and it can be deduced that no colour will enter into the definition of the set. But, as has been said, no such sophistication can be expected at the start, although there are children capable of such thinking. What is quite certain is that no particular benefit would accrue to children if the teacher "taught" children to work the problem out in this way. The point of such games is not simply to learn how to play them; it is rather that while learning how to play them, a certain amount of independent thinking is necessary. The games are played just in order to give children a chance to do such independent thinking; telling them how to play the games would do them out of this advantage, and would make the playing of the games pointless.

7. THE MATRIX GAME [1]

Children can be asked to tidy the set up. This is purposely very vague and children will sometimes make a vague attempt to make the pieces look tidy. The instructions can be further refined by telling them "Let us put all the large ones here, and all the small ones there. We'll start with the squares and then we'll go on to the oblongs, then the round ones and then the triangles" but it is advisable of course, to let the children come to these decisions by themselves. Maybe the 48 pieces are just a little too numerous for arranging conveniently in table form. Perhaps if a small number of pieces were systematically selected, and if they were told to tidy such sets up, the idea might occur to them more readily. If only thick large pieces were given there would be only 12 pieces, there being three colours and four shapes. It will not be long before children will arrange these in three rows of four pieces each, and then each row will contain the same colour pieces and probably they will be in the same order. In other words there will be a red row, a blue row and a yellow row, and probably there will be a square column, a triangle column, an oblong column and the round column. Having established this as a possibility then the sorting-out of the whole box in matrix or table form should be quite easy. Once the method of arranging has been selected and established, a game can be played, putting down only a certain number (i.e. a certain part of the matrix), and getting the children to make up the rest according to the rules that are seen to be operating by the pieces that have been put down. Of course, they can do this amongst themselves, and it can be made competitive. One person or one side can think of a rule and only put some of it into action. The other side can then attempt to reconstruct this rule

1. For more detailed comments and variations on the matrix game please see the appendix sections 1.12 and 1.13.

Tidying up the attribute blocks

Intersection of sets.   Three hoop Venn Diagram

Two difference game

by putting more pieces down. Again, wrongly placed pieces can be challenged and points can be awarded or subtracted as the case may be. If a rule which is different from the one thought of by the first group is operated by the second group, this should be allowed, as long as this different rule is consistent with the positions of the pieces already down.

One way of playing the game, which is really a cross between the domino game and the matrix game, is to tell children to vary the thickness from piece to piece along a row but keep the size constant. The instructions might run as follows : "Only put large pieces in this row, but have them thick, thin, thick, thin, etc...." Then a parallel row might be asked for, this time with only small pieces, starting again with thick, then thin, then thick then thin and so on. Children should be told that colours and shapes do not matter in this game, only the thickness and size.

Eventually a matrix such as this might be the result :

thick large	thin large	thick large	thin large	thick large	thin large
thick small	thin small	thick small	thin small	thick small	thin small
thick large	thin large	thick large	thin large	thick large	thin large
thick small	thin small	thick small	thin small	thick small	thin small

and so on.

In the "left-right" direction the size remains the same while the thickness alternates. In the "away-towards us" direction the thickness remains the same but the size alternates. It will not be long before some child notices that if a diagonal line is taken, then you change the thick-thin as well as the large-small.

This game is a forerunner of the transformation games, for in the "walks" in the three different directions we are engendering (i) size changes, (ii) thickness changes, (iii) size and thickness changes. It also introduces children to the idea that certain things are relevant sometimes and not at other times. In the games up till now, colours and shapes have always been relevant. Here they are irrelevant.

8. THE HOOP GAMES (VENN DIAGRAMS)
(See also the Cross-roads Game, p. 70 in the appendix.)

8.1. *The two-way hoop game*

Two wooden hoops may be put down on the floor so that one hoop overlaps the other hoop. Children can be told that, for example, inside one of the hoops must be put only the red pieces and that no red pieces must go outside, whilst inside the other hoop they must put only the oblongs, no oblongs being put outside this hoop. In the beginning children may take quite a while to decide what to do with the red oblongs. These will go, of course, on the part of the floor where the hoops overlap because this part is inside the red hoop and also inside the oblong hoop. The pieces which are neither red nor

33

oblongs must be left outside. This means that the 48 pieces will have been divided into four classes—the red oblongs, the red ones which are not oblongs, the oblongs which are not red, and those pieces which are neither red nor oblongs. This will be the first exercise which deals with the relationships which exist between "and" and "not".

The children should also be introduced to the situation where there is no block in the intersection set, and this can be set up by naming one hoop, say, "thick" and the other hoop, say, "thin", and so on. Many variations should be used in the naming of the hoops, and, later, it should be left to chance, by having piles of pieces of cardboard, each marked with the name of an attribute. These are shuffled and turned upside-down, and the children take a card, which decides the name of the hoop in each case.

These games can be played competitively, with players being entitled to a point or a counter, for each block placed correctly, and with every child entitled to "challenge" as before.

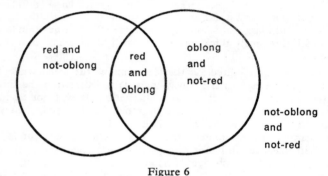

red and
not-oblong

red
and
oblong

oblong
and
not-red

not-oblong
and
not-red

Figure 6

This can also be played with the children in the classroom. A rope can be used which can be put round children that have certain attributes. For example we might take the children with black shoes on and invite all the children with black shoes on to go inside one loop of rope. We might say that all children with fair hair must go inside another loop of rope. It may take some time before the fair-haired children who happen to be wearing black shoes that day know where they have to go. There is often quite an argument about what should happen to such children. The black-shoes people want them to go with them and the fair-haired people want them to come with them too. Eventually it will be discovered that the two ropes can be put in such a way that they overlap, in which case the children who have fair hair and are wearing black shoes as well, can stand in the overlap between the two ropes. They will then be standing inside both ropes at the same time. This game can easily be extended to a game with three hoops of rope.

34

8.2. *The three-hoop game*

For this three hoops must be put down on the floor so that they overlap. Each hoop will be given a certain attribute. Perhaps one will be given a colour, another a shape and the third a thickness or a size. Let us say that the first one is "blue", the second one is "square" and the third one is "large". It must be explained that inside the first hoop must go all the blue things, that nothing blue must go outside and only blue things must go inside. The second hoop must contain all (and only) the square things and no square things are allowed outside. The third hoop must contain all (and only) the large things and no large things must go outside it. Points can again be given for pieces correctly placed and challenging encouraged as in the other games. It will be seen that this arrangement divides all the 48 things into eight classes, namely : the large blue squares, the not-large blue squares, the large not-blue squares, the large blue not-squares, the large not-blue not-squares, the blue not-large not-squares, the not-blue not-large squares and the not-large not-blue not-squares, the latter being left outside all three hoops. This sounds quite formidable before one has seen children doing it. Four-year-olds have been known to do it with practically no errors on just one set of instructions. Again, this game can be extended to other attributes and other objects so that again the logical relationships learnt in the games with the attribute blocks become easily transferable to other situations such as those involving attributes of people and later those of number or sets of numbers and so on.

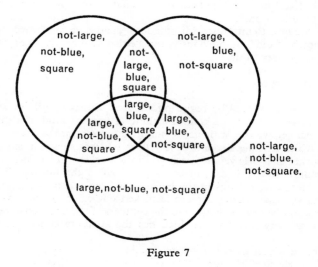

Figure 7

The game can also be played with four attributes. Teachers are reminded that it is impossible to draw four circles so that all the sixteen combinations of insides and outsides of these circles is represented by a region between arcs of such circles. This means that in order to play the game with four attributes, ropes might be necessary, to ensure that every combination of the four attributes and their negations has a "home", in which pieces with such combinations of attributes can rightly be placed. Alternatively chalkmarks may be made on the floor. The four-attribute game is much more difficult than the three-attribute game, and no particular educational purpose would be served by insisting that children learn to combine four attributes and their negations exhaustively.

If, however, children are keen to try their intellectual skill in this direction, they should not be discouraged.

9. DISJUNCTIONS

Introducing disjunctions—"Either-or" games

So far, when describing a block or a set of blocks, we have named the conjoint attributes in turn, joining the name of each attribute and the next with "and" or "and (understood)". There has been some small variation, but we have been following the same road when using negations, in that each attribute mentioned, either in the negative or the positive form, has been joined to the next word by "and". So "red and thick and square" is similar in form and construction to "not-red and not-thick and square". That is, we have been dealing with "conjunctions".

We are now to introduce "disjunctions", and here the "word signs" will not be "and", as previously, but "either ... or ...". Let us see how we go about this.

9.1. *Either-or games*

This can be played by requiring children to make a pile in which every piece is either one kind of a thing or another kind of a thing : for instance, we might instruct children to put into a bucket any piece which is *either* a square *or* is yellow. If it is square it can go in the bucket or if it is yellow it can go in the bucket. That means if it is a yellow square it can, of course, still go in the bucket. When every piece that belongs in the bucket has been put there, it will be true to say that whatever piece is picked out of the bucket will be either a square or be yellow. So the contents of the bucket will represent a set, any member of which has the attribute *either square or yellow*.

A piece which is in the bucket is, then, either square or yellow. This is perhaps a little sophisticated at first for children to understand but perhaps pieces can be taken out of the bucket and hidden and children can be asked "Is this either a square or yellow?" They will, of course, readily agree that it is. Then they can look at the piece and see which of the two it is or if it is both. They can be asked "Is it true that the piece I am holding is either a square or yellow?" They will readily say that it is indeed true and in fact when they look at it they will verify that it is true when they see which of the two it is or if it is both.

The next part of the game could be to ask children to pick from the bucket a piece which is not yellow. Of course, any piece which is not yellow is bound to be a square. All the not-yellow pieces will be picked out and the children will be surprised to find that they are all square. So the pieces in the bucket have the attribute : "if not yellow, then square". These can be put back into the bucket and children can be asked to pick pieces which are not squares. They will soon see that all pieces which are not squares are yellow. So every piece in the bucket has the property: "if not square, then yellow". This is yet another deduction which children will have made from an either-or statement, following upon the rudimentary deductions made while playing the Negation Game. It means that when an either-or situation exists then, an implication situation may be deduced. The either-or situation here is that everything in the bucket is "either a square or yellow". The implication situations are : "If not yellow, then square", "if not square then yellow". The implications are *deduced* from the either-or situation. The implications themselves are properties of the sets in the buckets and the deduction is not itself an implication. We have *deduced* an implication from an either-or attribute. This is the first time that a distinction will be made between a *deduction* and an *implication*.

It will be interesting to look at the pieces which are not in the bucket. These pieces are both not-yellow and not-square because all the yellow pieces as well as all the square pieces have been put into the bucket so that those that are not in the bucket are the pieces that are not-yellow and not-square. So the set which is left out of the bucket, is an "and" set. Those pieces which are not in the bucket have the attribute "not either-square-or-yellow" which we see now is the same attribute as "both not-square and not-yellow". Here again we have *deduced* an attribute from another attribute. One attribute is the negation of the either-or attribute and we see that this negation is an "and" attribute of the negations of the component attributes in the either-or attribute. The "not" of an either-or statement is the "and" of the negations of the statements which make up the either-or. "*Not* either square or yellow" is the same thing as "not square *and* not yellow".

Now this can be further complicated by constructing an either-or set in which there are already some negated attributes. We could say that we want people to put pieces in the bucket which are *either* blue *or* not-triangles. Anything blue can go into the bucket or anything that is not-triangle can go into the bucket. That means that if we pick out any triangle from the bucket it is bound to be blue, and if we pick out anything which is not blue from the bucket it is bound to be a non-triangle. Here again we are deducing implications from either-or attributes and generally learning to find our way about in the attribute calculus.

9.2. *Competitive version*

The above game can be made competitive in the same way as the other games by getting children to place the pieces one after the other in the bucket. Again each player is entitled to challenge the previous player and claim that the previous piece should not have been put in the bucket. When the bucket has been correctly filled, it can be decided that the children should issue commands which would involve certain other attributes than those included in the command. For instance, in the bucket which contained pieces which were either blue or non-triangles, is it possible to issue a command such as "Pick a piece out of the bucket which is so-and-so", in such a way that it will be certain that what has been picked out will have a certain other attribute which is not included in the command? There are, of course, two ways of doing this in the case of an either-or pile. In the case where every piece is either blue or a non-triangle, if a triangle is asked for then it will be blue. If a non-blue piece is asked for, it will be a non-triangle. If a blue piece is asked for, it will not necessarily be a triangle nor will it necessarily be a non-triangle. There are two ways of asking people to pick out pieces from an "either-or" pile in such a way as to ensure that an attribute not included in the command will be possessed by the pieces picked. For such commands we can choose from the two attributes and their negations. So there are four commands we can issue. (In the above case : (1) a blue, (2) a non-blue, (3) a triangle, (4) a non-triangle.) Now two of these commands will be successful and two will not ; i.e. two of them will imply certain other attributes and the other two will not. Therefore, the command "Pick out a triangle", will mean that the person will have picked out a blue one, but the command "Pick out a non-triangle", does not ensure either that a blue one will be picked or that a non-blue one will be picked. And so only those commands will score points which will inevitably imply a certain other attribute not included in the command. This will sharpen the children's reasoning and permit the formation of the realisations of the relationship between the either-or attributes and the if-then attributes.

To make the game even more difficult it would be possible to start from an "and" pile,—for example red *and* square—and pass on to the complement of this set which is *either* not-red *or* not-square. In this latter pile there are pieces that are either not-red or not-square or both. We can issue a command—e.g. "Pick out a red one"—and then of course it would also be a non-square. Or, we can issue a command "Pick out a square one", and then of course, it will also be a non-red, and so on. So the game can be made more difficult by starting further back at the "and" pile, instead of starting at the "either-or" pile itself. It will be remembered that every "and" pile has a complementary "either-or" pile, and every "either-or" pile has a complementary "and" pile. These are logical rules usually referred to as the de Morgan rules, after the mathematician of that name. Games can be played whose purpose would be the learning of the de Morgan relationships.

The "either-or" and "if-then" games can be played using verbal situations, once children have had sufficient practice with the blocks to enable them to apply these relationships to other situations. Children can be asked to think of "if-then" situations which apply to themselves without fail. One child might say, for instance : "If it rains, our garage leaks." We can suggest to him that if the garage was leaking one morning, could we say anything about it raining that morning? If the child says, "yes, it was raining", he needs further practice with concrete "if-then" situations. On the other hand if he says : "The man next door had the hose on", we shall know that he has learned about the non-invertibility of "if-then" situations. On the other hand if we suggest that the garage was not leaking, then it cannot have been raining, because we know that if it had been, then the garage would have leaked.

The development into more formal reasoning is left to the next stage of primary education.

9.3. *Complements of "either-or" piles*

Let us take an "either-or" pile ; for example,

Either red or circle.

Into this set would go all the pieces that are red as well as all the pieces that are round. In this way the attribute of being "either red or round", i.e. "either red or a circle" would be physically represented by the set consisting of these objects. Now what objects are in the complementary set? These are the blocks which are neither red nor round. Or putting it another way, the complementary set has in it the pieces which are both not-red and not-round.

Children could be asked to make the "red-or-round" set, and then see how they could describe the set of the blocks that were left out of the "red-or-round" set. We could ask "What can you say about every member of the set of blocks that are not in the "red-or-round" set?" Children would discover that every member of the complementary set is not-red. They would also discover that every member of the complementary set is not-round. Therefore every member of the complementary set is "both not-red and not-round".

Other "either-or" sets can be then constructed, and the complementary sets considered. The first child who can state *both* things that we can say of the members of the complementary set, wins the game and is then the next one to construct an "either-or" set. In this way children will realize that the complementary set of an "either-or" set is an "and" set. Some bright ones will even spot the fact that exactly the negations of the properties defining the "either-or" set have to be conjoined to define the complementary set. This is one of the de Morgan rules. If it is realized that the negation of a negation is the original attribute, then no difficulty will be experienced with the complementary sets of "either-or" sets such as "either yellow or not-triangle", "either not-blue or not-square", and so on.

For three-way "either-or-" games please see the appendix page 77.

9.4. *Complements of "and" piles*

Let us consider an "and" pile, such as for example "blue and square". What is the complementary set of this set? This set will consist of those blocks which are either not-blue or not-square. The question can be asked "What kind of pieces are there in the complementary set?" If nothing much is forthcoming, a little help can be given by asking "every piece is ..." stopping short of the little word "either", but eventually including it in the hint if need be. So it will eventually be realized that the property possessed by the complementary set of an "and" set can be expressed by "either-or"-ing the negations of the defining properties of the original set. In other words "NOT blue-*and*-square" is the same as saying "Either NOT-blue or NOT-square". The exercise can be turned into a game in the same way as the previous complement game.

10. TRANSFORMATION GAMES

10.1. *The copying game*

For this there must be two sets of blocks and two sides, each side having one set of blocks. Great care must be taken that the two sets are not mixed up. Therefore each side will have a complete set, no more and no less. The first kind of copying will, of course, be an identical form of copying i.e. one side makes some sort of building or any sort of construction with the blocks and the other side has to copy it exactly. Some five- and even six-year-olds find this really quite difficult. It is advisable to limit the number of pieces to be used to five or six for making the first construction. If a pattern is made by one side, the exact copying of the pattern does present some difficulty. To learn to do this would seem to help children to concentrate on the spatial relationships between the pieces and so would result in some important learning. Once children can do this, the copying can be made more complex : for example, it might be decided that the same building must be made but that every time a blue piece was put down by one side a red piece will be put down by the other, but that otherwise the same shape, size and thickness is to be used ; and similarly if a red piece is put down by one side then a blue piece of the same shape, size and thickness is to be put down by the other side. On the other hand a yellow piece which is put down by the first side is copied as an identical yellow piece by the other side. In other words the structure is copied exactly except that blue and red pieces are interchanged. The copying can of course be done in a different way, i.e. maybe even the first side can recopy the second side by choosing another colour combination. Very soon children will begin thinking of "cyclic" colour changes e.g. that blue should be copied as red, red should be copied as yellow, and yellow should be copied as blue, and so on.

There are various other obvious copying games that can be played : for example, large ones can be copied by small ones and small ones by large ones, or thick ones by thin ones and thin ones by thick ones, or both of these at the same time, and so on. The game can be made as complicated as the children wish and again become quite a challenging game. It is an important introduction to the idea of transformation and can even lead children to the realization of some of the properties of mathematical groups. If three groups are doing the copying game, playing in this case with three sets of attribute blocks, then A can build the building, B can copy this according to a certain rule, then C can copy B according to a certain other rule. The question can then be put to the children : "What is the rule which copies A into C ?" This will bring them into the domain of the theory of transformations. Of course, the shapes can be changed as well, and as there are four shapes there are many more possibilities that can be tried—for example, squares and triangles can be interchanged, and circles and oblongs, and so on. Four-way cyclic combinations can also be tried.

10.2. *Developments of the copying game*

It will be realized that the copying game contains in it the germs of much very advanced mathematical activity. The idea of transformation or function, which generates from one given situation a new situation, is included in these games. Further, the combination of such transformations is also included, as for example when group A's building is copied in a certain way by group B, and then group B's is copied in a certain other way by group C, the question of how group A's has been copied by group C arises. This is the combination of the two copyings. Perhaps at this stage instead of the word "copying" we might begin to use the word "transformation" in describing the games, though not yet with the children.

Take, for example, the transformation which turns blue into red and red into blue and leaves the yellow unaltered and the other transformation which copies everything identically. Clearly if we keep on doing one or the other of these transformations—maybe one of them several times over, then the other several times over, and so on—however many times we have performed a succession of such transformations the very last building can be obtained from the very first one still by just one of these transformations. This is because the copying simply copies i.e. all colours remain exactly the same, and the blue-red changeover simply changes blue into red and red into blue and leaves the yellow unchanged. So when this transformation has taken place twice we are back to the copying. Children will realize that one copying followed by a blue-red change will yield a total transformation of a blue-red change, and a blue-red change followed by another blue-red change will yield a copying transformation. Further, one copying transformation followed by another copying transformation is, of course, equivalent to a single copying transformation. Of course, it is not necessary to take a blue-red change and let the yellow remain the same. You may taken a red-yellow change and let the blue stay the same, or a blue-yellow change and let the red stay the same. It will be clear that there are just these three ways of constructing colour transformations of the kind just described.

10.3. *Cyclic games and inverses*

There are of course cyclic transformations; for example, red can be transformed into blue, blue into yellow and yellow into red in one transformation of a building into a second building. If this second building is then transformed into a third building—i.e. anything red in the second building is transformed into blue in the third building and anything blue in the second building is transformed into yellow in the third building, and anything yellow in the second building is transformed back into red in the third building—then what is the transformation which has taken place from the first building to the third building? It is now no longer the copying transformation. In other words, the pieces in the third building do not have the same colours as the corresponding pieces in the first building. It will be seen that the yellow ones of the first building have been turned into blue ones in the third, blue ones in the first building will have been turned into red ones in the third, and red ones in the first building will have been turned into yellow ones in the third. The transformation of the first building into the third is exactly the opposite of the transformation of the first building into the second. By this is meant that if we use this new, joint transformation after the first one we will get the copying transformation i.e. if we use the first transformation in turning our first building into a second building and then instead of using this same one again to obtain the third building we use the joint transformation to turn the second building into a third building, then the pieces of this third building will have the same colours as the corresponding pieces of the first one. This is obvious, because in the original transformation, red goes into blue, blue into yellow and yellow into red. In the joint transformation the yellow goes into blue, blue into red and red into yellow. In other words, everything goes back to what it was. Two such transformations which when applied one after the other yield the copying transformation, are called "inverses" of one another. Mathematics abounds in inverses. The use of inverse operations is a key-note towards understanding the relationships between operations such as addition and subtraction, multiplication and division, powers and roots, logarithms and antilogarithmes, and so on. If children encounter transformations and their inverses early in their school careers, it seems likely that when they come across the more difficult situations relating to addition and subtraction, multiplication and division, these situations will appear less difficult for them, as the relationships between inverse and direct transformations will be old friends.

10.4. *Combining games; tables of composites*

Naturally, very similar transformations can be obtained by the use of the other attributes. In fact, for the simple copying and change-over, possibly the thick and thin, or the large and small might be easier to handle although if these are presented at first then the road to generalization would appear to be more difficult. So it is suggested that the colour-changing be treated as the first kind of experience in transformations followed, possibly, by size- and thickness-changing operations. In the case of thickness there are two things one can do—one can copy everything exactly (which is the copying transformation) or one can simply "copy" a thin piece by the equivalent thick piece. In other words, in passing from building A to building B thick ones become thin ones and thin ones become thick ones, all other attributes being preserved.

There is no need to restrict the changes to thickness change. Size-change might in fact be easier to handle, especially for very young children, as a difference in size is more easily noticeable than a difference in thickness. In the size transformation, large ones become small, and small ones become large. When children have played around with thickness-change as well as with size-change, it might occur to them to change both attributes at the same time. In such a case, a large thick one would be changed into a small thin one, or a small thick one into a large thin one, and so on. Considering thickness and size, we now have four different transformations :

(C) Copying, (S) size-change, (T) thickness-change, (ST) thickness-and-size-change.

43

It will be interesting to see to what extent children are able to find the relationships between the above transformations. For example, if

	Building A	is transformed into	Building B	by size-change
and	Building B	is transformed into	Building C	by thickness-change, then
	Building A	is transformed into	Building C	by a thickness-and-size-change

or if

	Building A	is transformed into	Building B	by size-change
and	Building B	is transformed into	Building C	by size-and-thickness-change
then	Building A	is transformed into	Building C	by thickness-change.

in this second case, the size of each piece will have been changed twice, once from A to B, and a second time from B to C, and so every piece will have regained its original size. Thus the total change from A to C will be only a thickness-change.

It will be realized after a while that whichever two of the above four transformations are done, the equivalent single composite transformation will always be one of the four transformations listed.

It will be remembered that these changes have already occurred in the last form of the matrix game in section 7.

It will be seen that

(i) size-change, followed by size-change, restores the initial situation :

(ii) thickness-change, followed by thickness-change, also restores the initial situation :

(iii) size-and-thickness-change, followed by size-and-thickness-change, also restores the initial situation.

In other words any of these transformations, when repeated, restores the initial situation. Such a repetition of operations is therefore equivalent to a single copying operation.

It will also be easily verified that out of the three transformations

(S)   (T) and (ST)

any two performed one after the other, will be equivalent to the third one. Formally :

(ST) . (S) = (T), (S) . (T) = (ST), (ST) . (T) = (S) as well as
(S) . (ST) = (T), (T) . (S) = (ST), (T) . (ST) = (S)

The rule-structure which is exhibited by the set of these transformations is known as the *Klein-group*. The full table is as follows, as will easily be verified : (C = copy, T = thickness, S = size)

C . C = C	C . T = T	C . S = S	C . ST = ST
T . C = T	T . T = C	T . S = ST	T . ST = S
S . C = S	S . T = ST	S . S = C	S . ST = T
ST . C = ST	ST . T = S	ST . S = T	ST . ST = C

Figure 8

Similar games can also be played with colour-changes and shape-changes or any other kind of changes. For example, one transformation could be the one in which red and blue are interchanged and the yellow is preserved. This could be our colour-change. A shape-change might be the one in which squares and triangles are interchanged and in which circles and oblongs are interchanged. Our third transformation would be the one in which both of the above changes were made at the same time. If we also introduced the straight copying as a transformation, we should have a set of transformations which obeyed the same rules as far as their interrelations were concerned, as the rules shown in figure 8. Instead of size and thickness, we have simply varied colour and shape.

Actually a little more care needs to be taken to ensure that we obtain the same rules. It is necessary to pick transformations which when done twice, are equivalent to the copying transformation. This requirement is clearly met by our new colour-changing transformation, as well as by our shape-changing transformation. It will be instructive to construct the table for this new set of transformations and to verify that the two tables are in fact identical, apart from the names of the "moves".

10.5. *Further study of cyclic games*

We might consider the following cyclic transformation, using shapes only :

FIRST CYCLE : square into triangle, triangle into oblong
oblong into circle, circle into square

and then we might consider the cycle in the opposite sense, i.e.

SECOND CYCLE : square into circle circle into oblong
oblong into triangle triangle into square.

Clearly, applying the first cycle and then the second cycle, we restore the initial situation, as the second cycle undoes everything done by the first cycle. Similarly, if we start with applying the second cycle and follow this by applying the first cycle, we again restore the initial situation, as the first cycle likewise undoes everything done by the second cycle. The question will arise : "What happens when we use the same cycle twice over?" It will be easily verified that we obtain the transformation :

EXCHANGING : square into oblong, triangle into circle,
oblong into square, circle into triangle

which is seen to exchange squares and oblongs for each other, as well as triangles and circles for each other. It will likewise be seen that the second cycle when applied twice, will also yield for its composite the same exchanging transformation just described. Have we closed the game? Or shall we need, for example, to introduce a new transformation as the composite of the first cycle and the exchanging? Or for the second cycle and the exchanging? It will be seen on looking at figure 9 that the game is indeed closed.

If we use the following abbreviations :

C : copying, F : first cycle, S : second cycle, E : exchanging,
it will be verified that the relationships between the above transformations are expressed by the table below :

C . C = C	C . F = F	C . S = S	C . E = E
F . C = F	F . F = E	F . S = C	F . E = S
S . C = S	S . F = C	S . S = E	S . E = F
E . C = E	E . F = S	E . S = F	E . E = C

Figure 9

By the time children get as far as playing this game, they will have discovered the property of zero in addition, as well as the addition "facts" between the first few numbers. They can be asked to make a circle of numerals as shown in the figure 10.

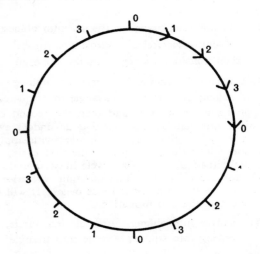

A cyclic number-game
with four numerals.

Fig. 10

The following "number game" may be played with this circle: start at any of the zeros, and take either

no steps, one step, two steps, or three steps, in the direction of the arrows.

Correspondingly we shall remain at numerals 0, 1, 2, or 3 respectively. Suppose we have taken one step, and we have come to rest at the numeral 1 next to the zero at which we started. Suppose we now take another step in the direction of the arrows. We shall reach the position denoted by a numeral 2. We could say that

$$1 + 1 = 2$$

This will correspond to F . F = E. But suppose we start at zero and take three steps. This takes us to a numeral 3. Suppose now that we take 3 more steps. We shall have reached a numeral 2. This means that in this "number game"

$$3 + 3 = 2$$

which corresponds to S . S = E in the transformation game.

These correspond to the facts that in the other game, i.e. in the transformation game, the successive application of the same cyclic transformation twice over, yields in each case the exchanging transformation as the composite. Perhaps the correspondence will be seen more clearly if it is set out formally, together with some of its applications, as will be found below:

Copying :   0 or the taking of no steps around the circle
First cycle :   1 or the taking of 1 step along the arrows
Exchanging :   2 or the taking of 2 steps along the arrows
Second cycle : 3 or the taking of 3 steps along the arrows.

| First cycle | followed by | First cycle | equivalent to | exchanging |
| 1 | + | 1 | = | 2 |

OR

| First cycle | followed by | Second cycle | equivalent to | copying |
| 1 | + | 3 | = | 0 |

OR

| Exchanging | followed by | First cycle | equivalent to | Second cycle |
| 2 | + | 1 | = | 3 |

and so on.

If division by 4 has been done, and remainders discussed, then children can be asked to classify numbers into four classes:

The 0-class, to this class belong the numbers which when divided by 4 leave remainder zero, i. e. the numbers divisible by 4.

The 1-class, to this class belong the numbers which when divided by 4 leave remainder 1.

The 2-class, to this class belong the numbers which when divided by 4 leave remainder 2.

The 3-class, to this class belong the numbers which when divided by 4 leave remainder 3.

It will be seen, for example, that a 1-class number added to another 1-class number, will yield a 2-class number. This can be expressed symbolically by writing $1 + 1 = 2$. Also a 1-class number added to a 3-class number, will yield a 0-class number and so on. This "adding-game" will be seen to be really the same game as the stepping round the numeral circle, as well as the same as the transformations we have been discussing.

The same game can be played by turning the children around. For example we can take a whole turn as one rule in the game, i.e. a child turns right round until he is back to where he was. The turn can be a spin about a vertical axis through the child, i.e. it can be a turn around about himself, or it can be a turn carried out by travelling all the way round a circle. Another move could be for the child to turn in a clockwise direction, i.e. towards his right hand, one quarter of a complete turn, i.e. through one right-angle. Another move could be that the child turns now anti-clockwise, i.e. towards his left hand, one quarter of a complete turn, i.e. again through one right-angle. The fourth move could be to get the child to turn half way round : whichever way he was facing, after a half turn he will be facing the opposite direction. So there are four moves in this "game"

(1) the whole turn, (2) quarter turn towards the child's right
(3) quarter turn towards the child's left, (4) half-turn.

It will be seen that these "moves" also combine together in exactly the same way as the 0, 1, 2, 3 game, the adding game described, and the transformation game with the two cyclic moves and the exchanging move in it. The transcription will be

0 corresponds to the whole turn
1 corresponds to quarter-turn towards child's right
2 corresponds to half-turn
3 corresponds to quarter-turn towards the child's left.

It should also be clear that another transcription would be obtained by making the 1 correspond to the left turn and the 3 to the right turn.

The correspondences with the exchanging game will be

Copying corresponds to the whole turn
First cycle corresponds to quarter-turn towards child's right
Exchanging corresponds to half-turn
Second cycle corresponds to quarter-turn towards the child's left.

Again another correct transcription would be obtained by making the first cycle correspond to the left-turn and the second cycle to the right-turn.

Village construction games

Intersection of sets. Three hoop Venn Diagram

« *Matching by size, thickness and colour* »
(photograph by Jan Dalman)

« *Village construction game* »
(photograph by Jan Dalman)

This game is a lead-up to the study of the remainders that we obtain when dividing numbers by 4. Likewise the games with the thickness change and copying, for example, lead up to the remainders that we obtain when we divide by 2, i.e. to the study of the properties of even and odd numbers. An even number, when divided by 2, leaves a remainder zero, an odd number, when divided by 2, leaves a remainder 1. These are the only possible remainders that we can obtain if we divide a natural number by 2. The rules obtained for combining the operations of thickness-change and of copying, are the same as the rules of adding odd and even numbers. We have the correspondences:

thickness-change   corresponds to   odd numbers
copying   corresponds to   even numbers.

For examples:

thickness-change followed by copying is equivalent to thickness-change and an odd number added to an even number is an odd number.

It can be verified that the correspondence works in all other cases as well.

Later on children will come across this very same structure when they begin to learn about positive and negative numbers. The multiplication of positive and negative numbers follows the same rules as the addition of even and odd numbers, or the combination of such transformations as the copying and the thickness change. Positive times positive giving positive, corresponds to copying followed by copying being a copying; negative times negative also giving positive, corresponds to a thickness-change followed by another thickness-change being equivalent to a copying. It will be again verified that the correspondence holds in all the other cases too.

If the children are young enough to appreciate "magic", they can be told that the transformations are magic that are performed by certain magic wands. Appropriate symbols can be drawn on these magic wands, such as, for example,

THICK   into   THIN
THIN   into   THICK

could be written on one wand. The word COPY could be written on another. In the case of colours, the actual colours could conveniently be drawn, or the words for these colours, if these are already familiar. Arrows can be placed between the colours in the directions of the change which any particular wand will perform. Children will readily invent new wands, each performing different types of magic, and the problems arising out of the relationships between their new wands will lead to much useful mathematical thinking.

49

11. THE LOGICAL SYMBOLS

As soon as children become aware of the properties of the logical connectives operating between attributes, i.e. connectives such as "and", "or", "not", and so on, it is advisable to introduce some sort of notation. One of the notations used in some parts of the world, introduced by Lukasziewicz, consists of the following symbols :

N is used for negation, i.e. for the word "not", as applied to an attribute,

K is used for the joining of two attributes by the word "and"
   (the K is placed in front of the two attributes to which it refers).

For example we might use the letter r to denote red, and the letter s to denote square. Then K r s would mean "red square". The letter K would mean the simultaneous application of the attributes "red", and of the attribute "square". N r would mean, "not red". N s would mean "not square", and so on. It is possible to negate compound attributes ; a negation such as N K r s would be possible : it would mean "not both red and square", and it would apply to any object that was not a red square, i. e. to either a not-red or to a not-square object.

Clearly we shall need a symbol for the "either ... or" connective ; this is usually the letter A (A for alternation). For example "either red or square" would be written A r s. This might refer to any piece in a bucket into which pieces have been placed that are either red or square pieces (or both, of course). If we wanted to express "either not-red or not-square" we would write A N r N s. It will be noticed that the N refers only to the attribute which it immediately precedes. If the letter N comes before a K symbol, for example, then it applies to the whole composite attribute. For example N K r s would mean the negation of the attribute K r s, K r s being the attribute that has been formed out of the attributes redness and squareness.

Games can be played, of the two-hoop or of the three-hoop types, and the symbols for the attributes of the pieces in the different regions may be put in by the children. For example, if we have a two-hoop game, in which one hoop is to contain the blue pieces and the other the square pieces, then the intersection will be K blue square, and the other insides of the hoops but outside the intersections, will be

K N blue square   K blue N square

The pieces that are left outside both hoops will have the attribute K N blue N square.

It will be realized that for example, K N blue N square can also be written as K N square N blue. These are different ways of expressing the same attribute.

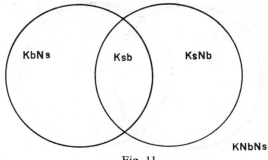

Fig. 11

This leads to some symbol games that can be played with the symbols themselves. This is only to be recommended if the ideas for which the symbols stand have been firmly established through the children's previous experiences. For example, an attribute may be constructed by means of the symbols, and then the corresponding set of blocks may be put out. Or a set of blocks may be put out and the corresponding attribute may be constructed by the children with the symbols. Having played this game, so as to make sure that the bridge between symbol and symbolized has been established, then games purely with the symbols may become possible. The attribute symbolizing a certain set of blocks may be put down and then the order in which the symbols have been placed can be changed. This may have one of three results :

one result may be that the resulting symbol is nonsense. For example the N may have been put at the end of the attribute-symbol. There is nothing for this N to refer to, since according to the rules each N refers to the attribute symbol that comes immediately after it ;

the other possibility is that the resulting symbol has some sense, but with reference to different attributes, i.e. it describes a different set of blocks ;

the final third possibility is that the changed symbol may be another way of expressing the same attribute. For example K red square is really expressing the same attribute as K square red. If a piece is red and square, it is also square and red.

It becomes quite challenging to require children to fill in the places in a three-hoop arrangement with the appropriate symbols, without putting in the pieces. Another game that can be played could be that a certain part of the three-hoop area, say one region of it, is filled in with blocks, and a card is put down face downwards, the rest of the children in the group having to guess what is on the card. Of course the symbol for the set put in the region will be on the card. There is not a unique solution to the problem of finding the symbols for the rest of the regions even if the hoops all must have "positive" names. For example take the following three-hoop arrangement :

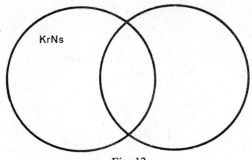

Fig. 12

According to the symbols, the region marked has been filled with the thin red pieces that are not square. The top left hoop could be red and the top right thin, or the other way round, the lower hoop being square. But there are other possibilities such as the top left hoop being red, the top right one being not square, and the lower one being not thin. A game could be played by two players A and B, A filling in one region with blocks and putting its symbol down face downwards ; this could be followed by B filling another region, possibly naming the hoops differently from A, but still consistently with how A filled his region. A will then fill a third region, possibly re-interpreting the names of the hoops, and so on. Each time a region is filled, the corresponding symbol is placed in that region but face downwards. Points may be awarded for correctly filled regions, correct symbols, and successful challenges. A challenge in this case is a claim by one player that the other player has filled a region inconsistently with the regions already filled.

Let us take an example from a two-hoop game to make the procedure clear. Supposing that two hoops are used and player A starts by filling in the left region as follows :

There are at this stage two possible interpretations of the hoops :
(1) left hoop is red,   right hoop is square
(2) left hoop is not-square,   right hoop is not-red.

Therefore there are two ways of filling in the overlapping region :
(a) either with the red squares, under the first interpretation,
(b) or with not-red not-squares, under the second interpretation.

Whichever one of these is done, there are no further alternative interpretations for the remainder of the game. In other words after the second region has been filled in, at any rate in this case, there are no further choices left for the players for the remainder of the game.

If, on the other hand, the second player fills the overlap with K s N r, i.e. with the squares that are not red, the first player could successfully challenge him. He could substantiate his challenge as follows :

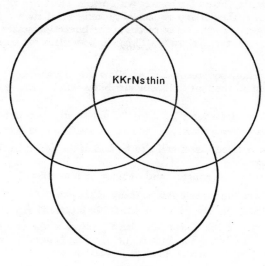

Fig. 13

"You have put some red pieces as well as some non-red pieces in the left hoop. This means that the left hoop cannot have a name to do with red. But you have also put square pieces as well as non-square pieces in the left hoop. This means that the left hoop cannot have a name to do with square. There are only four possible names for any hoop : red, non-red, square, non-square. The left-hand hoop cannot have any of these names, so it cannot have a name at all. You have made a mistake."

To substantiate a challenge in the case of the three-hoop game it would be necessary to show that some particular hoop cannot have a name by showing that each of the eight possible names has been made impossible by the previous player's move.

It will have been noticed that for joining three attributes with "and"-s, two K symbols or "and"-s are necessary. Each K refers to the attribute-symbols immediately after that K. For example in

K K r Ns thin, the first K refers to K r Ns and thin
                the second K refers to r and Ns.

The same attribute could have been therefore symbolized by the symbols

K thin K r Ns   or   K thin K Ns r   or   K K Ns r thin.

The same applies to multiple either-or symbols, i.e. A symbols. Other logical symbols in common use are

C   for   "if ... then"
E   for   "if and only if ... then"

For example, if we fill a bucket with pieces which are either yellow or not-square, then if any square is picked out of such a bucket, it will be yellow. So the set of pieces in the bucket possesses the attribute "if square, then yellow". This will be written for short as

C s y

If only yellow squares and non-yellow non-squares are put in the bucket, then all the four following attributes will be true of the set in the bucket:

(a) "if yellow then square",   (b) "if not-square then not-yellow",
(c) "if square then yellow",   (d) "if not-yellow then not-square"

It will be noticed that it can also be said of the pieces in the bucket that they are:

(e)   "yellow or not-square   and   square or not-yellow"

We can write the above symbolically as follows:

(a) C y s, (b) C Ns Ny, (c) C s y, (d) C Ny Ns, (e) K A y Ns A s Ny

In the last one the K (i.e. the "and") refers to the two attributes A y Ns and A s Ny. The first A (i.e. the first "either … or") refers to y and to Ns, the second A refers to s and Ny.

The short way of expressing the fact that the "if … then" attributes are true in both directions, is to say that in our bucketful

yellowness is equivalent to squareness, or in symbols

E y s

or   E s y.

It is suggested that this shorthand logical notation be developed very gradually. There would be little point in learning the techniques of manipulating this symbol system without being aware of what the symbols represented. There are, of course, alternative symbol systems used in logic. For example, some people use & for "and" and v for "or" and ∽ for "not". For example "both not red and square" would be written in the two symbol systems as

∽ r & s,   K Nr s,

whilst not (both red and square) would be written as

∽ (r & s),   N K r s.

It is seen that in the other symbol system brackets are necessary to distinguish certain attributes from certain others. In the system explained here, i.e. the N, K, A, C, E, system, no brackets are ever necessary.

The "logical" games that have been presented are not to be considered as exhaustive. A great many other games are possible, with or without the attribute blocks. On the other hand it must not be imagined that these logical games are given here to be handed on to children in a series of exercices much in the same way as the now happily old-fashioned unending series of monotonous "sums". Those responsible for the creation of children's mathematical environments i.e. in the last resort the practising teachers, must eventually take the responsibility for constructing such an environment for the children under their care in which mathematical thinking of a creative kind will continually take place. The suggestions given in this and in other chapters are intended as guide-lines to help teachers to construct such rich mathematical environments in which mathematical problems abound ; and, what is also important, in which the possibility always exists of finding the solutions to these problems by asking the pertinent questions. The questions should, as far as possible, be addressed to the environment itself, much as the scientist addresses his questions to Nature herself. The role of the teacher is to guide children in acquiring the skill to ask such questions in such ways that answers will be readily forthcoming from the environment. Formulating a problem is as important a part of learning as finding solutions to problems already formulated. It is often because we are unable to formulate our difficulties what we are unable to solve them.

The next booklet will take in the study of sets, and the bridge that must be built between the study of sets and the study of numbers. Naturally much of what is described in the next section will have to be studied alongside what has already been described in this one, for the study of sets is but another facet of the study of logic.

LESSONS AND GAMES LEADING
TO AN UNDERSTANDING OF LOGIC

The following games have been collected from many different sources but especially from the work done by William Hull, who was first to use "attribute blocks" as aids to the learning of Logic. Similar work has been done under our guidance at Cowandilla Infant School, in South Australia, and we are indebted to the teachers there, especially Mrs. D. M. Vick and Miss J. Hartnett, for some of the ideas that follow. Of necessity, a considerable number of the games described here were also included in the text, but it is necessary to repeat them in this section, so that a full series would be available in the one place.

Once again it should be understood that the work on Logic should be taken at the same time as that on sets and numbers. Some of the games included in these sections are very similar, but it should be understood that, if apparently repeated, the use and purpose will be different here from that of the previous section.

1. PRECEDING GAMES

Among the first games set down in each section of this appendix will be found a number of what we have, for want of a better name, called "concept" games, and such games should all be played before the set of attribute blocks is introduced. We refer to games designed to discover the extent of a child's previous experience and the extent to which concepts have developed, games to strengthen these basic concepts, games to introduce and strengthen the knowledge of colours, and so on. Teachers should turn first to these sections of the appendix and introduce as many of these kinds of games as possible, before proceeding with the games to follow.

The first two games described in the appendix of the booklet "Sets, Numbers and Powers" should also be played before these blocks are introduced. From these, the children will gain some understanding of the "universal set" (what we are talking about or considering today) and "set" (a "collection" of things forming part or the whole of the universal set).

So, our children, before they see the universal set of attribute blocks, will have been introduced to, or reminded of, such concepts as "round", "large", "small", and so on, other concepts such as "next to", "near", "in", a number of shapes and colours (including those we are to use here), and the names of most of these. They will also have had a little experience with several universal sets, such as the set of children in the room, of the furniture, of writing tools, and with sets chosen from within those universal sets, such as sets of boys, sets of girls, sets of children wearing black shoes. They will have had experiences with concrete materials—picking out sets of beads, buttons, toys, and similar everyday objects. While such experiences continue, teachers should be in no hurry to introduce these blocks, but their introduction should not be unduly delayed.

1. *Introducing the attribute blocks*

This game should be played before the children have seen what is in the box, which should be brought out, the lid removed, and then placed on a table, away from the children, so that they cannot see the contents. The children are asked to guess what is in the box. If they guess that it is "blocks", they are correct. Do not use too much time on this question, and help with hints if necessary.

Now the teacher takes out one block from the box, and shows it to the children, saying, "Here is a block. What kind of block is this?" The block will have, of course, four attributes, any one of which will be accepted, so that if, for instance, the teacher produced the "large, thick, blue square", the children could say it is a "large block", or a "blue block" or a "square block" or a "thick block", and the teacher will be satisfied with any one of these answers.

If a correct guess is made and a satisfactory answer given, the teacher asks, "Can you guess any other kind of block which might be in the box?" Let us suppose that a child guesses, "a red block", which is correct, because there are many red blocks in the box. The teacher will produce a red block, but will also take the opportunity of making it, say, a "red circle", so that the children are given a hint that there are circles in the box. Our next guess might then be, "a round block" and the teacher will again take the opportunity of introducing a new attribute, by producing, say, a "yellow circle" so that the children are reminded that there are yellow blocks in the box, and so on.

If there should come a time when no further guesses are made, the teacher may say, "Well, what kind of block is this?" Producing another block from the box, to get the game moving again, but it has been found that there is seldom need for this, as the class will usually guess names for every block in the box, without many hints. If the teacher gives encouragement when a child uses more than one name to guess the next block, such as saying, "a blue square" instead of just "a blue block", this tendency will build up as the game proceeds, but it must not be expected at this stage. One attribute alone is sufficient.

This game can be played again, a day or so later, so that the children are introduced to the blocks all over again, and so that the slower child can play a bigger part. This time it will proceed far more quickly. It might also be necessary to play it yet again, with the slower children only taking part.

2. *Free play with the blocks*

Ideally, each child should have his own full set of blocks, but, in the class situation, one full set among four children will suffice. (If you don't have sufficient blocks, some of the children can be engaged in another occupation.)

Now the children can be told, "Take out all the pieces and see what you can make with them." Or they might be asked, "What different kinds of things can you build with them?" or, "What different patterns can you make with them?" or, "Do you think you can make a secret pattern or a secret building that no-one has ever made before?"

The teacher should encourage, but not direct; should praise wherever possible, and might even help a little where necessary. A child who is slow to see what can be done, might be given a partner, without its being made obvious that he is being helped.

Each individual child should continue with this kind of activity until he tires, and asks for something different, and hints leading toward different activities can be found for those who tire quickly.

As each child or group of children become proficient at such building, the teacher begins to make suggestions. She may ask, "Can you make something like that, but with a flat roof?" or, "Do you think it would look better if there were more blue pieces in it?", and so on.

3. *Attribute discrimination*

The next few kinds of games are included to aid the children to identify the various blocks. At this stage, one attribute is treated at a time.

Building with one attribute discrimination, each child is asked to choose one shape and then to take out all the pieces of that shape, no matter whether they be of different size or colour. (It will be found that few children worry about thickness at this stage.) This means that, as there are four shapes, four children each have a heap from the universal set for this game. Each child now tries to build something, using only the blocks in front of him.

When the buildings have been completed, which will take only a few minutes, a "hiding game" can be played. One builder turns his back and another child takes a block from his building, and hides it. The builder turns around and tries to guess which piece has been taken. If the piece taken were a "large, thin, blue square" and his best answer is "a blue square", this should be accepted, but if the answer is "a square" this is not good enough as all of his pieces are squares. This "hiding game" could be continued until each child has had three turns at guessing the missing piece.

Now the children exchange shapes, which can be most easily done by merely changing places, so that the children move to the pieces, instead of the pieces being moved to the children. The building proceeds again, but each child is expected "not to copy" what was built with these pieces last time. Again the hiding game will be played.

These games should continue until each child has used each of the four shapes, and this will take more than one lesson.

If it is desired that these games be played competitively, each child can be given a number of counters. Every time he is able to guess which piece was taken from his building, he places one counter in front of him. If he can "give it a better name" he can get one bonus point. For instance, "a red square" would be worth one point, but "a large, red square" would gain two points. For the purpose of competition, a "game" is concluded when the children move to a new place. Usually, the winner will be obvious, but, if the game is close the teacher will decide the winner. It is not expected that the children will yet be able to count.

The same games can now be played with the pieces being divided according to colour, so we will have only three children dividing a universal set among them. In this case, each child takes all the pieces of the same colour and builds with them. The same kinds of hiding games will follow.

Similarly, the attribute can be changed to "size" and we have found it best to use teams of two children each, for these games. Two children take all of the large pieces between them, and build in co-operation. When the pieces are hidden, both players must turn their backs and each guesses in turn which piece has been taken.

In the same way, the attribute of "thickness" can be introduced and the same pairs of players can play the same kinds of games.

The main purpose of these games is to help the children to become used to the blocks with which they are playing, and to draw their attention to the various attributes.

4. *One attribute discrimination*—"Jumping Puddles"

This is a game played by a class, or a group of children, but like some of the other games it could be varied to suit an individual child. One child is to "take a parcel to grandma", who lives on the other side of the town, but it has been raining, so there will be "puddles" on the way, and these must be jumped. Some of the other children are selected to decide what puddles there are to be, and where they are to be placed. So, we may have a "square" puddle, an "oblong" puddle, a "red" puddle, and so on, with just one piece being placed in position to denote the puddle in each case. The messenger takes the

Fig. 14 Jumping Puddles

parcel, reaches the first puddle, names it, saying "the square puddle", jumps over it, reaches the second puddle, names it, saying "the oblong puddle", jumps over it, and so on, until the parcel is handed to grandma.

A new parcel is handed to another messenger, and another group of children is chosen, each of whom adds a piece to a puddle. That is, another square piece is added to the square puddle, another oblong piece is added to the oblong puddle, and so on. The messenger takes his parcel, names each puddle, jumps each puddle, and delivers his parcel.

With every new messenger a new piece is added to each puddle, and the game proceeds as before.

When the game is reconstructed the teacher encourages the building of some new kinds of puddles, including size and thickness among the attributes used. Where some children find a little difficulty with attribute discrimination, they are assisted by being given a partner to go with them, and so he is helped with the naming of the puddles.

5. *One attribute discrimination*—Musical guesses

The children are divided into four groups, one to deal with size, one with thickness, one with colour and one with shape. The teacher asks for about ten blocks to be placed in a hoop on the floor. This

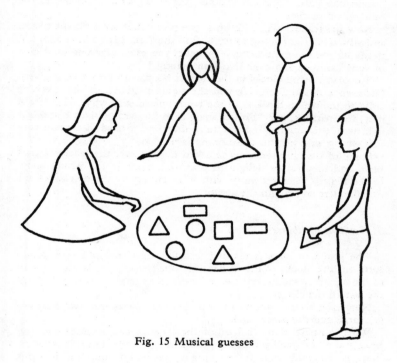

Fig. 15 Musical guesses

section of the game can give practice at selecting hoops by the given attributes.

Now, while the teacher plays a few bars of quick music, a previously chosen child puts any other block in the hoop, and runs back to his place. As the child selects the block he must make sure that every child can see it.

Now the teacher must guess which block was added, so she asks a child in one group, "What colour?", and a child in the next group, "What size?" and so on, until she is able to select the block.

When the teacher has found the block, it is left in the hoop and the game starts again with another selected child.

6. *One attribute discrimination*—Playing detectives

Four hoops are placed on the floor and some blocks of each shape are placed in each hoop, as the teacher names them. For instance, the teacher might say, "a large, blue triangle" and the children will put this in the "triangle hoop", and so on. The squares will all go in one hoop, the circles in another, the triangles in another and the oblongs in another.

Now the teacher will pick up a group of about six different blocks and will say, "I am going to try to find the right places for these, but if any of you see me making a mistake, you must give one loud clap of your hands to show me that I am wrong."

She places some blocks in the correct hoops and no signal is given, but then a mistake is made and the signal is given, so she asks one child to see which block is in the wrong place, and why. The child may, for instance, say "This triangle is in the wrong place because it is in with the squares." Sometimes they find it hard to explain why it is wrong, and helpful questioning is needed.

Some of the children may be asked to take over the teacher's part here, and they rather delight in putting a block in the wrong hoop, to see if they "can get away with it". However, the detectives are usually alert and sound the alarm.

7. *Conjoint attributes*

The group or class is divided into four sections, and each group sorts out the blocks so that it has only one shape—one section has all of the squares, another all the oblongs, another all the triangles and the last all the circles.

Now each section is asked to divide their blocks into two heaps—one large and the other small.

When all have done this, all of the large pieces are placed in one heap and all of small pieces are placed in the other, but this must be done by the children, in turn, taking a piece and naming it as it is put on the heap. For instance, the first child picks up a block and says, "a small square", the next child takes a pieces and says, "a large oblong" and so on. The conjoint attributes used in this case are size and shape.

Now the heap is divided again, into the four sections, using shape again as the attribute concerned. Now each section is asked once again to divide their pieces into two parts—this time, thick and thin. When all have done this, all of the thick pieces are placed in one heap, and all of the thin pieces are placed in the other, but again, each piece must be named as it is placed on the heap. In this case, the first child may say, "a thin square", and the second, "a thick square" and so on. The conjoint attributes in this case will be thickness and shape.

For the next of these games the children will again start by dividing the blocks into their shapes, but now each section will divide its blocks into three parts, with one colour in each small heap. Now the teacher will ask that all the red pieces be placed "there". Once again, before a block is put on the heap, it must be named, so the first child may say, "a blue triangle", the next "a yellow circle" and so on. The conjoint attributes in this case will be colour and shape.

It will be obvious to teachers that various combinations, each of two attributes, should be used in their turn, so that children will become accustomed to using two attributes to describe each piece.

8. *Conjoint attributes*—Making a stew

We start this game with a hoop, or a circle to represent the stock pot, and the blocks will represent the ingredients. Now the teacher says, "I am making a stew here, and I would like to put a big, yellow turnip into it. Will you please hand me a big, yellow turnip?" A child finds a large, yellow block, which is put in the "stew". The teacher pretends to stir and taste the stew. She makes a grimace and says, "We will have to put something else in it. Will you please give me a small, red carrot?" A child hands her a small, red block, and it, too is added, but with the same result. Now she asks for "some, large, blue onions", and then a "thin, red radish" and so on. Every time the teacher adds a block, and "stirs the stew", she grimaces, until she is satisfied that the game should end. Then she smiles and says that the stew is "just right".

A variation of this game suggests that we are making a "fruit cake".

9. *Further Conjoint attributes*

Sixteen children are required to play the next game. The box of attribute blocks is emptied onto the floor in front of them and four children divide the pieces according to shape—one child taking blocks of one shape, and so on. When this has been done, two children from each group are asked to divide each heap into two sections— "large" and "small"—and so we now have eight heaps. Then, two more children are asked to divide each heap again, this time into "thick" and "thin". We will now have sixteen heaps, each of three blocks, in front of sixteen children.

Now the teacher discusses the various ways of naming the blocks with the children. It is agreed that there are four ways of naming each piece, but for the purposes of this game at least three are required. Each child now plays a piece in his turn, by placing it on a central heap, while naming it with at least three "names". So the first child takes a piece, names it by saying, "a large, thick, red block", or a "small, thin square" and so on. If a child uses more than the three attributes required, this should be allowed.

As the children become used to this kind of game, they will divide the blocks by using the attributes in different order, and, when naming the blocks, the children will be told that they can use "all except colour", or "all except shape" and so on.

This game can be played competitively if required, by allowing each child, who successfully does as he is asked, to take a counter on each occasion. The child who has the most counters at the end of the game is decided by the teacher to be the winner.

Fig. 16   The block in the bag

10. *Conjoint attributes*—What is in the bag?

Before this game commences the children are asked to decide upon an order of naming—preferably size, thickness, colour and shape—which has already been taking shape in the previous game. Now, one child will take charge of the game, having a box of blocks near him—but the blocks will be hidden from the other children. He will also have a cloth bag, with a draw string, or a piece of rag large enough to hold the largest block. He places any block in the bag, or wraps it in the rag, and hands it to the first child, who can feel it and try to guess some of its attributes. Of course, size, shape and thickness can be discovered, but colour must be guessed in the early stages.

The child in charge hands the wrapped block to another child and asks, "What can you tell me about this block?" The child may answer,

"I think it is a large, thin, red circle." (The attribute "red" will, of course, have to be a pure guess at this stage.) For every attribute correctly guessed the child will be allowed to take one counter from the box.

When a piece has been played, it is placed in the middle of the table so that the players can see it. As the game proceeds it can help them to decide about, say, colour. If, for instance, the player can feel that the block in the bag is a "large, thick triangle", and the player can see one or two large, thick triangles on the table, he will be helped when guessing the colour of the block in the bag.

11. *Blocks with certain attributes*

This is a very simple game for which all of the blocks are dropped on the floor, in any order and in any place, so long as all players can see them. One player then asks, "Who will find me the small, thin blue oblong?" and the player who finds the piece puts it in a special place, takes a counter and asks for the next piece. The game goes on until all the pieces have been found.

The blocks are again put on the floor, and the first player asks, "How many triangles altogether?" When he gets an answer, it is checked by gathering together all the triangles and checking them. The player who gave the right answer may now ask, "How many red circles are there?" and the same procedure is observed. Maybe the next question is "How many small blocks are there?" In each case the blocks are returned to the floor when they have been checked.

These kinds of "quizzes" allow the children to gain experience both with the blocks and with the naming of blocks by attributes. At this stage, perhaps the first is the more important game.

12. *The Matrix Game*—"Tidying up the set"

This game has been described in the text, on page 32. All the pieces in the universal set are placed on the table or on the floor, and the teacher asks the children. "Will you please tidy them up so that we will be able to find any piece easily and quickly?" Usually the children will then start to "sort the blocks out", putting all of one shape near one another, and arranging these again in some order. If, however, this is not sufficient, a further instruction may be required, such as, "Suppose we put the large ones here, and the small ones there, starting with the squares, then the circles, then the oblongs and then the triangles." This will be made easier if the floor or tabletop has been marked out with chalk in the form of a grid. When this game has been completed properly we will find that the blocks are arranged in "columns" and in "rows", and that, if we follow a line in one direction, we will find, perhaps, all of the red pieces, and in

65

another line, maybe in the other direction, all the square pieces, and so on.

It is possible that very young children may find 48 pieces too many to arrange for the first time, so we have frequently started with only

Tidying the Set

Colour

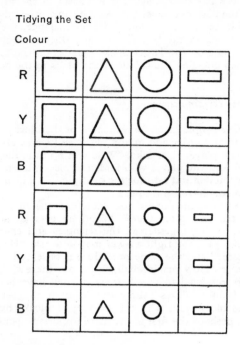

Matrix - Using thick blocks

Fig. 17

twelve pieces, confining ourselves to colour and shape only. This means that we can give one child all of the large, thin blocks, another all of the large, thick blocks, another all of the small thin blocks, and a fourth all of the small, thick blocks. In this case, the arrangement will be easy, as they will have to arrange only, say, "columns" of the three colours, and "rows" (across them) of the four shapes. So, in our "red column" we may have, in order, a square, then an oblong, then a circle and then a triangle. As we have only one of each, this will be easy. Now, if we complete our arrangement and look across the "square row", we will see that we have, say, a red square, then a yellow square and then a blue square, and so on.

If we are going to proceed in stages, the second stage should see only two divisions of the universal set, with one-half of the class, or group, having all of the large pieces, and the other all of the small pieces. From the first pattern they will see that they now have to decide where to put the thick pieces and the thin pieces. Are they going to keep the first pattern, and put another pattern down next to it, or are they going to alternate the rows? For example, if we read across our "square row" are we going to have a thick, red square, then a thick, red oblong, then a thick, red circle, then a thick, red triangle, then a thin, red square, then a thin, red oblong, then a thin, red circle and then a thin, red triangle, or are we going to have our two squares next to one another, first the thick and then the thin, and so on? However, so long as the children manage to get the blocks arranged in "table form", so that each piece can be easily found, it does not much matter which method is decided upon.

When this has been done, all of the pieces will be arranged in the one pattern—the arrangement of small pieces from one group being included in the arrangement of the large pieces from the other group. However, the children should not be limited to only one game with this kind of arrangement. Various different arrangements should be tried.

13. *More with matrices*

To start this game the teacher puts four or five pieces in position on the "grid". Let us suppose that the teacher decides that we will have an arrangement reversing the one suggested for the last game, that the "rows" ("horizontal" lines) should be used for shapes, and the "columns" ("vertical" lines) should be used for colours. Now, if the teacher puts down, say, the blue square and the blue oblong, the red triangle, the yellow circle and the yellow square, the child will have sufficient evidence of the kind of matrix that is to be completed. Once again, it might be best if this game is played with only one size at first, and then duplicated. The children may be introduced to the new word "matrix" if the teacher wishes, so long as all he needs to know is that it is a pattern in which all the blocks along one vertical line are of the same colour and all the blocks along a horizontal line are of the same shape, or are similar to each other in any one way.

When the matrix has been completed the children can play the "Hiding Game" again. That is, the group of children turn their backs and one child removes and hides one or more pieces from the matrix. The children turn about and try to name the pieces that have been hidden. Again, this game can be played competitively, with each successful child taking a counter.

Another game of this kind can be played in which one child, or one group, thinks of the "rule" which is going to set the pattern of their matrix and puts down a few blocks, but keeps the rule secret. The other child, or the other group, then tries to build the matrix according to the rule. In some cases, the builders do not keep exactly to the rule which the other group thought out, but, if they make a regular matrix, their blocks are allowed to stay as correct.

In another matrix game, the number of squares in the pattern are limited, so that there are spaces for only, say, twelve blocks, and the

Complete the Matrix

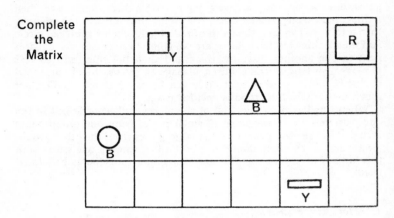

Use only thick or only thin pieces

Fig. 18

players are asked to build up a matrix, using only the twelve squares, but placing all of the blocks. It is obvious that some pieces must then be placed on top of one another, but, once again, the order, from bottom to top, in this third dimension, must be kept the same. For example, if the square containing the red squares has the large thick block at the bottom, then the large thin block, then the small thick block and the small thin block on top, all of the other blocks must be arranged in the same order.

14. *Naming the pieces*

In this game one child tries to name all of the pieces in the universal set. As each is named the piece is placed on the table by a second child, in such a way that a matrix is formed. This arrangement will help the first child to remember the pieces still to come.

At the next stage the blocks, though produced when named, are placed on the table, but not arranged as a matrix.

The third stage sees the child naming the pieces, but these are not now placed on the table. As each piece is named it is placed where the "namer" cannot see it, and so is not assisted.

It is obvious that these games can be played competitively, with credit being given for each block correctly named.

15. *Naming by "not"*

For this series of games the children will require a number of cards, on some of which will be marked the names of attributes, and on others these names will be preceded by the word "not". These are shuffled, and the players in the first game pick up the top card. Let us suppose that this is marked, "oblong". The child or group must now pick out every piece which is in the shape of an oblong, and by this heap will be placed the name oblong. Now the teacher will ask, "What can we call the other heap?" The answer is, of course, "not oblong", but the children may not be able to state this yet.

For the next game the teacher will see that the card is marked with the word "not". Let us suppose that this card is marked "not-square". Now the children will put in one heap every piece which is not square, leaving the other pieces in another heap. As previously, the label "not-square" is placed by the first selected heap. Now the teacher may ask, "What can we call the other heap?" At first the children will not realise it, but soon, some child will notice that all the pieces in this heap are "square", so the two heaps will now be named "square" and "not square". Perhaps the teacher will now remind the children of the previous game, where the heap picked out was "oblong" and she will ask the children if they can now give a name to the second heap. Now they will agree that these blocks are "not-oblong". (It may be necessary to do the actual work again before all the children realise this.)

The next game starts with the children being asked, perhaps, to make a heap of all of the "blue" blocks, and the other heap will have to be named, using the word "not". Of course, this will be the heap of "not-blue" blocks, and so on.

When the children are asked to select the heap of "thick" blocks and to name the other heap, using the word "not", the answer will, of course, be "not-thick". Then the teacher might ask the children, "Is there another name that we could give to this heap?" and the answer will be "thin". The same will apply to "large" and "small".

Many games should be played with the children picking out the complementary sets, and naming them with the use of the word "not", so that the children become accustomed to this way of naming pieces. They must understand, though they may not be able to state in so many words, that every time they pick out the set of, say "yellow blocks", they have, at the same time, picked out the set of "not-yellow blocks".

The cards are shuffled, one is taken in each game, and the two complementary sets are decided by what is on the card.

16. Conjunctions—The Cross-roads Game

For this game the teacher will mark out several "roads" with chalk, and on each of these, she will put a notice, to show what is to be allowed on that special road. So, we might have the "blue road", the "triangle road", the "thick road", the "small road", and so on. The children practise placing their blocks on the right road, having been told, for instance, that on the "blue road" must be placed all the blocks which are blue, that no other block is to be put there, and that no blue block is to be put anywhere else. Each road is filled in its turn, and the children become used to these "roads" representing certain attributes fully.

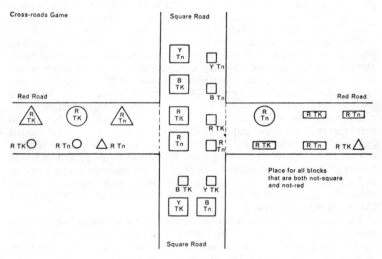

Fig. 19   Cross-roads Game

When the children have had practice at filling one road at a time, the teacher will introduce the "cross-roads". She may, for instance, draw the "blue road" crossing the "triangle road" and she may ask the children to take turns at picking up the pieces and putting them in their proper places. Now, this is not easy. If the first child, for instance, picks up a "red square", it is found not to be blue and not to be a triangle, so it cannot go on either road. A special place is found for these pieces which do not fit on our diagram. The next player might pick up a "blue square", which must, of course, go on the "blue road", and the next player might have a "red triangle" which must go on the "triangle road" and so on, until a player picks

70

up a "blue triangle". Now he must decide where this block must go. Being blue, it must go on the "blue road" and, being triangle, it must go on the "triangle road". This usually causes some concern until the player decides that this block must go at the cross-roads, where it is on both roads.

It will be seen that every block has its proper place—either on the "blue road", "the triangle road" or the "cross-roads", or in the special place made for blocks that cannot be placed on either road. Each block is either blue but not a triangle, or a triangle but not-blue, or both blue and triangle, or it is both not-blue and not-triangle and must be left off our roads. So we have introduced "conjunctions", shown by the need for the word "and" in the naming of the set of blocks, when we find the blocks for our cross-roads—"both blue and triangle".

Another pair of cross-roads will be built, perhaps using "red" and "square" for our attributes, and this might be followed by "large" and "thin" and so on. It is possible, of course, for us to have a pair of cross-roads where there are no blocks. This would happen if we made our roads, say, "yellow" and "blue", as there are no blocks which are "both yellow and blue". One or two examples of this should be shown, so that the children will know that it is possible, but should not be stressed too much.

These games, too, can be played competitively, with every child who plays a block properly being given a counter.

17. *Village construction games*

The hoop games so far have used individual blocks but now we shall deal with sets of blocks, which is a little different. These games commence in much the same way as did our games with Venn Diagrams, with which they must not be confused. The children are asked to place, say three, hoops separately on the floor. Each is marked with a colour, one being "red", another "blue" and the third "yellow" and all red blocks must be placed in the red hoop, all blue blocks in the blue hoop and all yellow blocks in the yellow hoop. This exercise can be varied by naming the hoops, "circle", "triangle", "square" and "oblong" and so on. Each block, or heap of blocks, is a "building".

Now we place two of these hoops on top of one another, and we label one hoop, say, "red" and the other hoop "blue". Once again the children make "buildings", but each building must consist of both red and blue blocks and they may be of as many "storeys" as the children decide to build. (This idea of building in storeys, or making piles, should also be practised with the single rings. Perhaps the teacher might ask for the same number of two storey buildings as one-storey buildings, and so on.) It will be noted that where the blocks are in both the red and the blue ring, a building using both red and blue pieces is required. When we were dealing with separate blocks, as in the Venn Diagrams, we could, of course, have no single block which was both red and blue, and so we would have an empty set in such circumstances.

At the third stage two hoops are placed on the floor, in such a way that they overlap, so that there is a section within both hoops at the same time. If we call one hoop the "red" hoop, and the other the "blue" hoop, there will be a section in which all houses built must be made of red blocks only, a section in which we must build with blue blocks only, and the common section, where each building must be constructed of both red and blue blocks. The children should first practise with the basic requirements, and then they might try adding some special rules of their own. Perhaps, the combined red-and-blue buildings will be made to be of equal numbers of each coloured block, or we may have a building height limit of two stories in the single-colour sections, and of four stories in the two-colour section, or we may decide to have as many buildings as possible, or as few buildings as possible (while taking heed of height limits in various sections) and so on. Some of these rules might be applied at the same time.

Two-Hoop Village Construction Games—Sets of Blocks

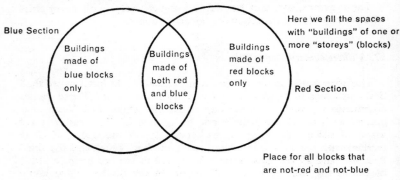

Blue Section

Buildings made of blue blocks only

Buildings made of both red and blue blocks

Buildings made of red blocks only

Here we fill the spaces with "buildings" of one or more "storeys" (blocks)

Red Section

Place for all blocks that are not-red and not-blue

Fig. 20

Let us suppose that we have our red and blue hoops, and that our special rules say that no building may be of more than two storeys, and that there must not be more two-storey buildings than one-storey buildings. Of course, every building in the "both red-and-blue" section must be of two storeys, and the children might begin by building some buildings there. In the "red only" section and the "blue only" section buildings may be of either two-storey or one-storey, so we might start by building some one storey buildings there. Now we might change our minds, and join some of these one-storey buildings together to make two-storey buildings, but we must make sure that there are always more one-storey buildings than two-storey buildings.

Or we may start again, and this time our special rule might say that there are to be no one-storey buildings at all, and that, in the "both red and blue" section every building must be of four-storeys. Other rules may be made and the children will find it great fun trying to obey the rules, and then answering the teacher's questions about what they have built.

18. *From blocks to sets of blocks*

For our next game we will use three intersecting hoops, each of which must cross both of the others. Let us suppose that these hoops are labelled "red", "blue" and "yellow" (though they might just as easily have been named "square", "circle" and "oblong"). This time the children will find a section where buildings must be of red blocks only, another of blue blocks only and a third of yellow blocks only. In the intersections there will be a section for buildings of both red and blue blocks, a section for buildings of both red and yellow blocks and a section for buildings of both blue and yellow blocks—and in these sections the houses must be of at least two storeys. There will also be one section for buildings of red and blue and yellow blocks, and here the houses must be of at least three storeys. As a first game the children will be free to fill the sections by building houses of whatever sizes they decide, so long as they follow the rules, and so long as no section is left empty. This game should be repeated, using other names for the hoops, before we proceed.

Of course, we do not need to use hoops for our divisions, and the diagram shows one way in which the area has been divided up, using

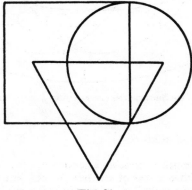

Fig. 21

a chalk diagram on the floor. This diagram also saves "naming the hoops" as we have used the circle, the square and the triangle, and the blocks to be used in each section are of the same shape as the shape we have drawn. So, if we have drawn a triangle (instead of using a hoop) we know that all of the triangle blocks must be found somewhere inside the large triangle on the floor, and so on. This has been found to be of assistance where children are poor readers. Our children repeat the game using this kind of diagram.

Here we have practised the "three-hoop village construction game" and we have varied the shapes of the sections. Again we can add extra rules for the children to follow. Maybe we can make a special rule that there must be as many three storey buildings as possible, or, in another game we may make the rule that there must be as many one storey buildings as possible, and so on.

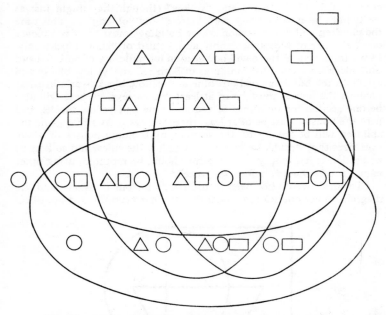

Fig. 22 *Village construction games – four hoop – sets of blocks.*

19. *Symbolisation in words*

This is not so much a game as a reminder. So far we have been playing games with our sets of attribute blocks, but little or nothing has been said about verbalisation by the children. In fact, so long as they have been able to show that they understood what they were doing, by doing it, we have been well satisfied. There is a great danger in a "too early, and too adult" verbalisation, as the children tend to confuse a glib, but little understood, set of words, with real understanding. They think that the former is what we want of them.

However, by the time they have reached this stage, the children, or the majority of them, will be able to put into words, or symbolise, what they have done, or what they are doing. For example, in a Venn Diagram, consisting of two hoops, labelled "red" and "square", they should be able to explain that the set of blocks which they have rejected are "not-red and not-square" that the intersection of the sets will be filled by blocks which are "both red and square", or merely, "red and square", and that the other sections are filled with pieces which are "red and not-square" and "square and not-red", respectively. In the earlier games the children learned to name each block through its attributes, so that they could say what the block was, "large, thin, blue oblong" and so on, so this newly required verbalisation is merely an extension of that requirement, but requiring the development of other concepts.

Some of these games should be repeated now, both for revision purposes, and so that the children can practise this "symbolisation in words"—at this stage required orally, and not in writing.

20. "Not" games

In addition to this normal kind of naming required as part of verbalisation, children need to be reminded of names for pieces or for sets of pieces which include the word "not" in the name. Therefore we will return to a previous kind of game and use a variation to give practice with this. This is the "Please may I have" kind of game, for which, it will be remembered, the children were divided into two teams sitting at opposite ends of the table. Half the pieces from the universal set of attribute blocks are placed on each end of the table and some kind of barrier is erected across the middle of the table so that neither team can see what is on the other side. Now team members take turns, alternating from team to team, to ask for any block which is not to be seen at their own end of the table.

The difference this time is that every block for which a player asks must be described using the word "not", before any attribute mentioned. Care must be used in asking for a piece in this way, as, for instance, a "not-large, not-thin, red square" is very different from a "not-large, not-thin, not-red square" and is different again from a "not-large, not-thin, not-red, not-square".

It is probably best, in the first game, to require only one attribute to be preceded by "not", and this will probably mean that children will use "not-small" instead of "large", or "not-large" for "small". The second game can require two attributes to be preceded by "not" and, this time, the players will probably use "not-thin" instead of "thick" and "not-thick" instead of "thin". So they will ask for a "not-large, not-thick, red circle" if they want a "small, thin, red circle". The next stage is more difficult, as we have more than two choices, so if we ask for a "not-red circle" we can get either a "blue circle" or a "yellow circle", and if we ask for a "not-large, not-thin, not-red circle" we must be given either the "small, thick, blue circle" or the "small, thick, yellow circle", so there must be more practice with this special kind of game.

At the next stage the choice is even greater, for, if we ask for a "not-circle" there is a choice of a "square", a "triangle" or an "oblong".

Once again, a piece once asked for and handed over, cannot be asked for again. When the children have again had practice at naming separate blocks, using the word "not" in the naming, they will find it easier to handle the naming of sets by the same method, so this game should be used to help with symbolisation in words.

21. Venn Diagrams played with "not"

Now let us return to our Venn Diagrams. As we have since played the village construction games, it might be best to play one or two three-hoop games to remind the children that we are again using single blocks and not sets of blocks. Now, our new game requires each hoop to be labelled using the word "not". Let us suppose that, in our first three-hoop game we ask for "not-red", "not-large" and "not-square" blocks.

It must now be remembered that all the pieces which are "not-red" must go into the "not-red hoop", and that they must not be placed anywhere else, so we will find that every blue and every yellow piece will be found in the "not-red hoop". Looking at our "not-large hoop" we know that, if a piece is "not-large" it must be small, so we must expect to find all of the small pieces in the "not-large hoop". Some of these pieces will be red and so cannot also go into the "not-red hoop", but the other pieces are both "not-red and not-large" and will be inside both hoops at the same time—in the intersection. In our "not-square hoop" we must expect to find all the circles, oblongs and triangles, because all these are "not-square". The various intersections will soon be decided.

This time we will have divided our universal set of attribute blocks into a new set of sets. We will have a subset in which the pieces are "not-red, not-large and not-square", one in which the pieces are "not-red and not-large", another of "not-large and not-square", another of "not-red and not-square", and others which are just "not-red", "not-large" and "not-square". Some of these subsets will overlap. Outside the hoops will be the rejected blocks which, in this case, will be of "large, red, squares" only.

Though the children can cope with this exercise, they find both the selection and the naming of their sets difficult, until they have had a good deal of practice. If, in the beginning, they seem to be lost, it should be preceded by some extra practice with complementary sets. This will involve the simple division of the universal set into two sections in each case, say, the "red" pieces, and its complement, the "not-red" pieces, or the "square" pieces, and its complement, the "not-square" pieces, and so on.

22. *More symbolisation in words*

We start this game with a heap of cards, on half of which is the word "not", while the rest of the cards are blank. A child picks up a block from the attribute box, and at the same time, picks up four cards from the top of the pack. Let us suppose that he has picked up the "large, thin, yellow circle" and that his cards read, in this order—"blank", "not", "blank", "not". This means that he can name his piece using the word "not" to name the second and fourth attribute. He will, perhaps, describe this block as, "large, not-thick, yellow, not-square".

At first the game is played orally only, and then we use the cards from the twenty-questions game so that the player not only names his block, as required, but also puts down the cards so that others can read what he has said.

Once again, points may be awarded for success, and challenges should be allowed. In all of these games it is best to allow discussion among players, all on the same level, so that they can "argue out" any points on which they disagree, rather than having the teacher take part at too early a stage.

23. *Three-way "either ... or ..." games*

There is no reason, of course, why we should stop at two choices when we use the "either ... or ..." method of making a set. We could, for instance, play this game "three ways". As an example, let us decide that in our bucket we will put the pieces that are "either red or thick or oblong". It will be easily seen that the pile of pieces in the complementary set will have to be "not-red and not-thick and not-oblong", so these will be the blue and yellow, thin, squares, circles and triangles.

What can we discover about the pieces in the bucket by asking our questions? If we ask the children to pick up a piece which is red, what do we know about it? Must it be thick? Must it be oblong? The answer to both questions is, of course, "No". But, if we ask the children to pick out a piece which is "not-red", what do we know about it? This time we will know that it is either thick or oblong. The same will apply to our questions about a piece which is "thick" or "not-thick", or "oblong" or "not-oblong". Try these for yourselves and see what you discover.

Discover whether the De Morgan rules still work in this situation, and then use the word "not" to describe some of your "either ... or ..." attributes.

List of Centres affiliated to the International Study Group for Mathematics Learning.

Leicestershire Mathematics Project.

Secretary J. S. Friis, *Leicestershire Education Committee, Education Department, Grey Friars, Leicester, England.*

Surrey Mathematics Research Group.

Secretary A. E. Adams, *Surrey County Council, Education Dpt. County Hall, Kingston-upon-Thames, Surrey.*

National Foundation for Educational Research for England and Wales.

Secretary and Director Dr. W. D. Wall, *79, Wimpole St., London, W. 1.*

C.E.P.A.M., Centre français d'Études du Processus d'Apprentissage en Mathématique.

Secretary R. Biemel, *65, rue Claude-Bernard, Paris 5.*

Sherbrooke Mathematics Project.

Secretary Z. P. Dienes, *University of Sherbrooke, Canada.*

Institut Rousseau.

Secretary S. Roller, *Palais Wilson, Genève.*

Florence Psychology Institute.

Secretary and Director Alberto Marzi, *Cia della Colonna, 17, Firenze.*

Budapest Mathematics Project.

Secretary Tomas Vargá, *6-8 Muzeum körút, Budapest, VIII.*

Philippines Mathematics Research Group.

Secretary Ron Carlisle, *Peace Corps, Baguio City, Republic of the Philippines.*

Adelaide Mathematics Project.

Secretary E. W. Golding, *Cowandilla Demonstration School, South Australia.*

Hilo Mathematics Research Group.
Secretary Mary Matayoshi, *Book Nook, Hilo, Hawaii.*

Minnesota School Mathematics Center.
Secretary and Director Paul Rosenbloom, *University of Minnesota, Minneapolis, Minn.*

Madison Project.
Secretary and Director Robert Davis, *Webster College, St. Louis, Missouri.*

Institute of mathematics in the Social Sciences.
Secretary and Director Patrick Suppes, *Stanford University, Stanford, California.*

Australian Council for Educational Research.
Secretary S. Dunn, *Melbourne, Australia.*

US Independent Schools Research Group.
Secretary William Hull, *40, Reservoir Street, Cambridge, Mass.*

Central Office of ISGML.
Secretary Adrian Sanford, *200, California Avenue, Palo Alto, California.*

The bulletin of the ISGML appears quarterly and is available to individual or corporate members ; U.N.E.S.C.O. is providing some initial assistance towards production costs, and also cooperating in establishing a wider information service.

DEPT. *Education*
O.N. 3609
PRICE 50p
ACCN. No. Misc. P. 370/146
COPY 2

Printed by E.S.A., Harlow, Essex.